The Taiping Revolution

By the Compilation Group
for the "History
of Modern China"
Series

FOREIGN LANGUAGES PRESS
PEKING 1976

Publisher's Note

The Taiping Revolution (1851-64) is one of several booklets translated from the "History of Modern China" Series, Shanghai People's Publishing House. Others are: *The Opium War (1840-42), The Reform Movement of 1898, The Yi Ho Tuan Movement of 1900* and *The Revolution of 1911.* All were compiled by members of the history departments of Futan University and Shanghai Teachers' University. Some editorial changes have been made in the English version.

First edition   1976
Printed in the People's Republic of China

Bust of Hung Hsiu-chuan.

Hung Hsiu-chuan's old home in Kuanlupu Village,
Huahsien County, Kwangtung Province.

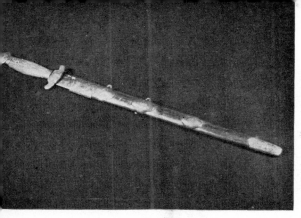

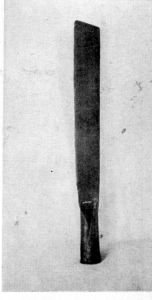

Swords used by the Taipings during the Chintien Uprising.

Cannon used by the Taiping Army.

Site of the Taiping Camp at Chintien.

Front cover of the *New Guide to Government*.

Front cover and a page from the *Heavenly Land System*.

堂間有被逃壞心腸者亦欲跟隨他走斯
時
救世主天兄基督統衆天使咸集
天父上主皇上帝大發聖旨凡高天人有跟隨妖魔
頭走者個個要捉囘凡有奸心幫妖者及
一切偷闖之妖魔仔個個要驅逐下去又
推勘妖魔作怪之由總追究孔丘教人之
書多錯

答他主亦斥孔丘曰爾作出這樣書教人
爾這樣會作書乎孔丘見高天人人歸咎
他他便私逃下天欲與妖魔頭偕走
天父上主皇上帝即差主同天使追孔丘將孔丘捆
綁解見
天父上主皇上帝怒甚命天使鞭撻他孔丘跪在
天父上主皇上帝
天兄基督前再三討饒鞭撻甚多孔丘哀求不已

Two pages from the *Taiping Tien Jih* (*Taiping Heavenly Days*). This book demolished Confucius who was worshipped as a "sage" by the feudal ruling class. It exposed the erroneous ideas of the Confucian canons, thus inspiring the working people to rise up in revolt.

A furious cannonade by the Taiping forces against the Ching war-junks encircling the Heavenly Capital.

During the Taiping Revolution, a number of foreigners served
with the Taiping Army. In December 1863, Lin-le, an Englishman friendly to the Taipings, helped repulse the Ching water
forces at Wusih with the *Firefly*, an armed steamer captured
from the "Ever-Victorious Army."

Contents

The Eve of the Tempest

After the Opium War of 1840, the new aggression of foreign capitalism in addition to the old feudal oppression made the lives of the people in China more difficult than ever. The contradictions in Chinese society sharpened, giving rise to crises.

During the Opium War, the British invaders did a lot of looting and extorting. Their booty included a large amount of silver plundered from many different places. On top of this they extorted the huge sum of 21,000,000 silver dollars from China as a war indemnity. If the damage done by the invaders and the war expenditure of the Ching government are also considered, the total cost of the war to China can be seen to have been even greater. This shocking burden in its entirety fell directly or indirectly on the shoulders of the people.

Even before the war, the spread of opium had already become a serious problem. The Opium

War started as a struggle between those who wished to sell opium and those who wished to ban it. After the war, the British and American invaders used Hongkong quite openly as a base for the opium trade, pouring opium in ever-increasing quantities into every coastal port of China. By the early 1850s, import of opium had reached 50,000-60,000 chests per annum. As opium was usually paid for in silver, 20,000,000 to 30,000,000 taels of silver flowed out of China each year. When Hung Hsiu-chuan rose in revolt, he bitterly denounced the Ching government for "wasting tens of millions of taels in gold and silver for opium." It was intolerable to the Chinese people that precious money should be spent on such harmful stuff.

The increasing outflow of silver aggravated the problem of the rising price of silver in terms of copper. The exchange rate between silver and copper cash, originally around 1,000 cash per tael of silver, had risen to 1,600 cash per tael by 1840, and to 2,200 or 2,300 cash per tael by 1850, an increase of more than 100 per cent. Peasants and handicraft workers were paid for their labour power or their products in copper cash at rates which did not rise. When they paid their taxes however, they had either to pay in silver, or to be assessed in silver. Even if the rate of the taxes had remained unchanged, their tax burden would have been more than double its former level. In fact, as the silver price was forced up even further artificially, and extra duties were often imposed, people frequently had to pay as much as 8,000 or 9,000, and even 10,000 copper cash for a tael of silver.

After the opening of the ports of Shanghai, Ningpo, Amoy, Foochow and Canton to foreign trade under the terms of the Treaty of Nanking (1842), foreign cotton textiles and other consumer goods poured in. The total value of the merchandise imported from Britain in 1842 was £ 969,381, by 1845 it was already £ 2,394,827, of which £ 99,958 was spent on cotton yarn and £ 1,635,183 on cotton goods. Owing to the resistance of China's self-sufficient natural economy and the effect on ordinary trade of the great outflow of silver for opium, China's foreign trade then declined for several successive years. But imported foreign textiles usurped the place of Chinese native-made cotton goods, and drove handicraft productions out of the market. By the mid-1840s, there were no longer good sales for cotton goods from Chekiang or Kiangsu, and stocks of native-made cloth were piling up in Fukien. The regions of Sungkiang and Taitsang in Kiangsu Province, once the most prosperous centres of native textiles, had only half their former volume of trade. This tendency gradually spread from the coastal regions and areas near the great rivers to the interior. China's old social-economic order was destroyed, handicraft manufacture went into decline and the path to industrial development was blocked. Large numbers of peasants and handicraft workers went bankrupt or became unemployed.

As Karl Marx so truly said of the Opium War in China: **"The tribute to be paid to England after the unfortunate war of 1840, the great unproductive consumption of opium, the drain of the precious metals by this trade, the destructive influence of foreign competition on native manufactures, the demoralized condition of the public administration, produced two things: the old taxation became more burdensome and harassing, and new taxation was added to the old."***

To pay the war indemnity and make up for its own shortage of silver, the Ching government not only extracted all the silver which it could get from the provinces by saying that the indemnity burden must be shared, under the pretext of "raising funds," it imposed endless miscellaneous levies, and both taxes and prices rose. The land and poll tax was the chief means by which the Ching govern-

---

* Karl Marx: "Revolution in China and in Europe."

4

ment squeezed the people. It supplied three quarters of the total government revenue, and in the period between 1841 and 1849 it increased by more than three million silver taels. Salt was for everyone an indispensable daily necessity. The official price for Changlu salt was fixed at between 16 and 24 copper cash per catty; by 1846 in places near the salt-producing area, it cost 33 or 34 cash, while in more distant regions it was as much as 60 or 70 cash. Indeed the payment of all sorts of taxes and duties cost the people many times what they theoretically had to pay if the discount on the official exchange rate and the bribes extorted by the Ching officials are allowed for. When people could not afford to pay, the local officials tried to force them to by every means at their disposal, even flogging and imprisoning them. Even Tseng Kuo-fan, a reactionary Ching official, admitted what was going on in his memorial to the Emperor in 1850: "Soldiers and government servants are sent out pursuing and compelling them day and night. They are whipped all over the court-house until they are covered with bleeding wounds."

To annex land and to plunder through the ownership of land were the basic means by which the landlord class carried out its ruthless exploitation of the peasantry in feudal society. Some decades before the Opium War, there was a saying:

"In those land-grabbing families, one man owns a hundred men's houses, one family owns a hundred families' land." The ownership of land and wealth gradually became more and more concentrated while the majority of people suffered in poverty. Following the Opium War, the social and economic order of China was violently shaken by foreign capitalism. Officials became greedier, trying harder than ever to lay their hands on silver, and with the same desire, landlords kept raising both money rent and mortgage rates and demanding all payments to be made in silver, while wealthy merchants and usurers manipulated the exchange of copper for silver and extended loans on which interest compounded daily. Under this intense exploitation large numbers of peasants lost what little cultivated land they had and became ever more impoverished. Even some minor landlords were on the brink of ruin, and landownership became more concentrated than ever. This concentration of landownership developed swiftly everywhere. In 120 years prior to the Opium War, a big landlord family called Meng, of Changchiu County in Shantung Province, bought only 46 *mu** of land in seven separate transactions. Between 1840 and 1850 this family bought land

---

* 1 *mu* is 1/15 hectare or roughly 1/6 acre.

15 times in all, totalling more than 196 *mu*. In Kueiping, Kueihsien, Pingnan, Hsiangchow and Luchuan of Kwangsi Province, most of the land belonged to landlords, many of whom possessed from a few hundred to several thousand *mu*, collecting rents of hundreds of thousands to a million catties of grain. This was a microcosm of the whole country. Everywhere there were landlords with over 3,000 *mu* of land. Still bigger landlords possessed as much as 10,000, 100,000 or even a million *mu* of land. Nationally, 70 or 80 per cent of the land was concentrated in the hands of the landlord class, which formed only a small minority of the nation's population.

So foreign capitalist aggression, added to the growing contradictions inherent in feudal society itself, gave rise to a dramatic intensification of the contradictions in Chinese society. The Tien Ti Hui (Heaven and Earth Society), a secret society of a popular, anti-dynastic nature, also known as the San Ho Hui (Triads) or San Tien Hui, whose members included peasants, handicraft workers, urban and rural labourers and vagrants, made this proclamation when it rose against the Ching government. "Throughout the Empire, rapacious officials are worse than bandits, and the corrupt mandarins of the public offices are no better than wolves and tigers. The crimes committed by the rich are left unpunished, and the wrongs of the poor never redressed. Deprived of their means of support, the people are plunged into the darkest depths of suffering." Chen Kai, leader of the Tien Ti Hui in Kwangtung Province said in his confession: "After the peace negotiations with the aliens (meaning the negotiations which led up to the Treaty of Nanking in which the Ching government surrendered to the British invaders), opium smokers have increased in great numbers. Large quantities of foreign goods have flooded in, and ordinary people do not know what is going on. They see that customs barriers are being built everywhere and the government compels them to be submissive to the aliens. The world has greatly altered, and people, having neither money nor food, sink into sorrow and grief." From their personal experience, such leaders were able to express in simple language the absolute antagonism between the people and their rulers.

Where there is oppression, there is resistance. In the 1840s there were uprisings of peasants and handicraft workers everywhere, and the minority nationalities also rebelled. In the space of 10 years there were well over 100 uprisings, ranging from struggles against the payment of levies, taxes and rents, and the delivery of grain to landlords, to assaults on cities, and the occupation of territory.

Most of these uprisings were initiated and organized by the popular, anti-dynastic secret societies such as the Pai Lien Chiao ("White Lotus" Sect) and the Tien Li Chiao (Heavenly Reason Sect) in north China, the Nien in Honan, Anhwei and Shantung, and the Chai Chiao (Society of Vegetarians) in Szechuan, Hunan, Kiangsi, Chekiang, Fukien and other provinces. The biggest of these secret societies and the one which led most uprisings was the Tien Ti Hui, which had spread all along the Yangtze and throughout the southern provinces. The secret societies had existed for a long time as a vehicle of popular dissent, but they became far more active after the Opium War, showing that the greater the oppression, the stronger the impetus to revolt. It was oppression that compelled the people to make revolution.

The provinces of Kwangsi, Kwangtung and Hunan were the scene of the most important of these armed uprisings, and the revolutionary forces soon concentrated themselves in Kwangsi. These three provinces, especially Kwangtung, had been the most directly affected by the Opium War and, after it, suffered most from the problem of discharged soldiers. This was also the region in which the Tien Ti Hui had for long organized people against the Ching. The ranks of the Tien Ti Hui were thus swelled both by the unemployed

9

and by homeless discharged soldiers. Furthermore, there was famine in this region for several successive years, so thousands of hungry, destitute people flocked to join. Rebellion, therefore, blazed up in all three provinces, and in Kwangsi where the rule of the Ching was comparatively weak, the sparks took hold and spread until the blaze became a prairie fire.

In 1847, Lei Tsai-hao, the leader of the Tien Ti Hui in Hsining, Hunan, and Li Shih-teh in Chuanchow, Kwangsi, rose in revolt on the Hunan-Kwangsi border. They attacked Chuanchow and fought against the Ching troops for two months with support from Tien Ti Hui groups in Kwangsi and Hunan.

In 1848, the insurrections led by the Tien Ti Hui in Kwangsi reached a climax. Chang Chia-hsiang led a revolt at Hengshan; his troops increased to well over 10,000, and were active around Chinchow, Lingshan, Kueihsien, Hengshan and other places on the Kwangtung-Kwangsi border. Later Chang Chia-hsiang surrendered to the Ching troops and became a traitor. Chen Ya-kuei organized an armed force of several thousand among the peasants at Chinchow in Kwangtung and Pinchow in Kwangsi and led a revolt at Wuhsuan. Having taken the two county towns of Hsiujen and Lipu in central Kwangsi, they advanced on Hsiangchow,

Wuhsuan and Kueihsien and were still fighting at the outbreak of the Taiping Revolution. Chang Chao and his men led a rising of boat people at Wuchow. Good at fighting on water, they soon took over the main waterways in Kwangsi.

In 1849, after the death of Lei Tsai-hao, one of his subordinates, Li Yuan-fa, led a rising at Hsinhua in Hunan, took the county town by storm, killed the county magistrate, broke into the granaries and opened the jails, shaking the complacency of the landlord class. Afterwards, they gained the mountain forests of the Hunan-Kwangsi border, breaking through the blockade of the landlord army, and their numbers increased to 4,000 to 5,000. They marched on into Kwangsi, and fought at Junghsien, Yungning, Yungfu, Yangshuo, Lipu and Hsiujen. There was a severe famine in Kwangsi that year. Hundreds and thousands of famine refugees with nowhere to go to, came and joined the Tien Ti Hui. Scores of such peasant insurrections broke out, each with several hundred to several thousand participants. They captured many cities and much territory.

As the 1850s opened, the ruling class was very alarmed by the revolutionary situation in Kwangsi. The officials petitioned the Emperor, who gave instructions for "investigations" to be carried out. There were frightened complaints about the growing number of "robbers and bandits" in Kwangsi, of whom the "bandits of Shang Ti Hui, a clamorous accumulation of 10,000 men," were the most dreaded. This Shang Ti Hui was none other than the Pai Shang Ti Hui (Society for the Worship of God), a revolutionary organization guided by Hung Hsiu-chuan.

Hung Hsiu-chuan was born into a peasant family in Kuanlupu Village, about 50 kilometres north of Canton, in Huahsien County, Kwangtung Province, on January 1, 1814. As a child, he helped his father and elder brother with the farm work, studying at the same time. At 18 he became a village school teacher, a rural intellectual who sympathized with the people's suffering and maintained close ties with the poor peasants. He sat the official examination at Canton several times to get a *hsiutsai* (a low degree in the imperial examination system) but was failed each time. This was the period of great popular unrest because of the oppressive rule of the Ching dynasty and the national humiliation of the Opium War. Influenced both by the shock of his own failures and by that of China's defeat, Hung Hsiu-chuan began step by step to take the revolutionary road.

In his article "On the People's Democratic Dictatorship," Chairman Mao said: **"From the time of China's defeat in the Opium War of 1840, Chinese progressives went through untold hardships in their quest for truth from the Western countries."*** Hung Hsiu-chuan was one of the earliest of China's progressives to look to the West for truth.

Before the Opium War, merchants and missionaries from the capitalist countries of the West were already active in China's coastal regions. The merchants carried opium with them while the missionaries brought the spiritual opium of the Christian religion. Canton was one of the first places to be affected.

In 1836 when Hung Hsiu-chuan was taking one of the examinations in Canton, he saw missionaries preaching and distributing religious books and tracts in the street. He took one entitled *Good Words for Exhorting the Age* compiled by Liang Fa, a Chinese Christian convert who had been assistant pastor to the British missionary Robert Morrison. The latter was the first Protestant

---

*Mao Tsetung: *Selected Works,* Eng. ed., Foreign Languages Press, Peking, 1969, Vol. IV, p. 412.

clergyman to come to China, though the Catholics had come earlier. He arrived in Canton in 1807 and also toured Macao, Malacca and other places. Planning to use his religion against China he learned the language and made the first complete translation of the Bible into Chinese. Liang Fa's book, *Good Words for Exhorting the Age* was in fact just extracts and stories from this Bible with annotations. It was published in nine volumes and ran to about 100,000 characters. Hung Hsiu-chuan took the books home, glanced over them and laid them aside. The following year he failed the official examination yet again. Upset and furious, he fell ill and as he lapsed into fits of delirium on his sickbed, he called on God and repudiated Confucius, the "sage" of the feudal ruling class.* He

* Confucius, a native of the State of Lu (present-day Shantung), was born in the last years of the Spring and Autumn Period (770-476 B.C.), the second son in his family. A thinker of the declining slave-owning aristocracy, he was the founder of the Confucian school of thought. Living in a period of great social upheaval during the collapse of the slave system and the rise of feudalism, Confucius dedicated his life to retrieving the former. He concocted a whole system of reactionary ideology with "jen" (benevolence) as its core, and advocated "restraining oneself and returning to the rites." — a programme for restoring the old order. He taught the idea of the "mandate of heaven" and preached apriorism through such fallacies as "life and death are predestined, and riches and honours come from heaven," and that some people are "born with knowledge." In his reac-

said, "The devils are making trouble" because "most of the canons taught by Confucius are absurd." Sometimes he would rave, "Kill the devils, kill them." He also recited the lines from his own poem: "Grasp the power to rule over Heaven and Earth; kill the evil to protect the righteous and relieve the distress of the people." Hung Hsiu-chuan's identification with religion enabled him to use Christian tenets to claim that he was sent by Heaven on a mission. This was his preparation for the revolutionary cause of "killing the evil to protect the righteous" and of wiping out injustice among men.

Hung Hsiu-chuan remained in his home village for the next few years, earning his living as a teacher. In 1843, he made his last attempt at the official examinations. The defeat of the Ching government in the Opium War exposed its military and political decadence to the world. Hung Hsiu-chuan then abandoned any idea of making his career through the feudal bureaucratic examination

---

tionary educational ideas he demonstrated a deep contempt for productive labour, declaring that "he who excels in learning can be an official." For some 2,000 years from the Han dynasty on, in China's feudal and semi-feudal, semi-colonial society, Confucius' reactionary ideology, embellished and developed by the rulers of the various regimes, was used to shield reactionary rule and shackle the working people's minds.

system and resolved to overthrow the Ching government. He wrote: "At the moment I am idle like a fish leaping in a deep pool as I bide my time for men to congregate." These lines again revealed his great desire for circumstances to allow him to take part in a revolution. With his classmate Feng Yun-shan and his cousin Hung Jen-kan, he looked at the book, *Good Words for Exhorting the Age*, which he had laid aside for so long, searching it for some grand ideal. The religious baptism described in the book did in fact inspire them to organize and they established in their village one of the earliest groups of the Pai Shang Ti Hui (Society for the Worship of God). Hung Hsiu-chuan assigned himself the role of God's son and Christ's brother who had come to earth to save mankind. Feng Yun-shan, who also taught in a Huahsien village school, became Hung Hsiu-chuan's close comrade and helped organize the society.

The aim of *Good Words for Exhorting the Age*, as of the other religious books, was to paralyse the people's will to rebel against the system under which the world was ruled by the exploiting classes. By preaching that people should revere some so-called "creator" or "the only true God," and teaching that "real happiness exists not on earth but only in Heaven," and that people should love their enemies, such books attempted to induce people to seek their happiness in the next world, not in this one. Hung Hsiu-chuan, however, interpreted the religious tracts differently. He considered that God was good but that all the other idols which people worshipped were demons. Why shouldn't the peasants then ally themselves with God against Confucius, the King of Hell, the emperors and the other devils? Since all people were born equal as the sons and daughters of God, why shouldn't the peasants rise up and fight for the equality of which they had so long been deprived? So the Society, when stripped of its religious mantle, was actually a revolutionary organization advocating an anti-religious philosophy of struggle. Many of Hung Hsiu-chuan's poems were not paeans to God but fervent outpourings of his revolutionary fighting will. Here is one example.

> Wielding a sword three feet long, to conquer mountains and rivers strong;
> Within the four seas, home is everywhere; let's drink a cup of common happiness and joy.
> All monsters and devils we'll capture and cast into Hell;
> Traitors and blood-suckers will all be suppressed, caught in the snare of Heaven.
> Our land, east, west, north and south firmly consolidated,

> The sun, moon and stars all sing in triumphant
> chorus.
> The tigers howl, the dragons snarl — that brightens
> heaven and earth;
> Where peace rules, endless happiness will reign.

The message is clear: state power is secured by the sword, happiness is realized only through hard struggle, and only by capturing all demons and by suppressing traitors and blood-suckers, can peace be brought to the world. Hung Hsiu-chuan always carried with him a three-foot-long sword which he had forged inscribed with the words "For Slaying Demons." The first line of the poem shows his intentions in fairly concrete terms. Subsequently, in spite of the opposition of the rural gentry and elders of the clans, he smashed the ancestral tablets of Confucius set up for worship in schools, thus challenging the feudal intellectual authority which had been held for 2,000 years as sacred and inviolable. This was Hung Hsiu-chuan's first step in the struggle.

In the spring of 1844, Hung Hsiu-chuan and Feng Yun-shan went to the Kueiping-Kueihsien area of Kwangsi Province where they worked energetically for several months recruiting followers at Tzuku Village in Kueihsien. They organized a group of more than 100, the first revolutionary fighters who were later to fight in the

Taiping Army. Hung Hsiu-chuan returned to Kwangtung that winter as little was happening in Kwangsi, while Feng Yun-shan stayed behind to take charge there.

In 1845-46, while Hung Hsiu-chuan was teaching in his home village, he wrote *Doctrines on Salvation, Doctrines on Awakening the World, Doctrines on Arousing the World* and other revolutionary articles based on the demands of the peasants, in which he combined the Western religious idea of "equality" with the Great Harmony concept of ancient China. Hung Hsiu-chuan exposed the darkness of his society, saying: "All love and hatred stem from selfishness," and expressed a longing for the society of great harmony as envisaged in ancient China. Contrasting the ideal society of mutual love and understanding with the contemporary world filled with rivalry and brutality, he wrote of his detestation of the social order of the time and his aim of establishing an ideal kingdom on earth in its stead. Hung Hsiu-chuan further clarified his opposition to the feudal system of ranks, feudal class oppression and autocracy in the lines: "All under Heaven have the same Heavenly Father and so are of one family," "what reason is there for the Emperor to grasp everything in his own hands?" "Within the four seas all are brothers and the Heavenly Father cherishes all as sons." Hung Hsiu-chuan thought also that all men under Heaven were brothers and all women, sisters, and there should be no walls or bounds between people, nor should people trample over one another. In other words, the world of inequality, full of mutual hatred, rivalry, brutality and slaughter, should not be allowed to exist. He stood for equality between countries, between peoples, between men and women, between the rich and the poor — an ideal filled with militant courage in absolute opposition to feudalism.

In his *Doctrines on Arousing the World,* Hung Hsiu-chuan condemned the injury and torture inflicted on people by the supernatural system ranging from the Monster King of Hell, down to the various spirits and demons of the underworld. He identified these as the Ching Emperor and his subordinates and officials against whom the people should revolt, as they were the source of all evil. Hung Hsiu-chuan thus pointed out the target of the struggle and expressed his determination to stand together with the people to smash and sweep away all the idols of feudalism.

In March 1847, Hung Hsiu-chuan learned that the American missionary Issachar J. Roberts was in Canton and, eager to seek for truth, went with Hung Jen-kan to see him. But the missionary, though ardent in propagating his religion to dope the Chinese people, did not trust Hung Hsiu-chuan and would not receive him into the Church. During his two-months' stay, Hung Hsiu-chuan studied the Bible. Finally he fell out with Roberts and left the place. Later, evaluating the religion of the Taiping Heavenly Kingdom, the missionary said that they were "bent on making their burlesque religious pretensions serve their political purposes."* That was right. Their basic difference was in their different political aims. Hung Hsiu-chuan returned to Kwangsi and joined Feng Yun-shan, who was active at Tzuchingshan in Kueiping County, and both immersed themselves in the popular struggle.

Kwangsi was a province slandered by the land-lords as being "infested with bandits." This was their class view of the sharp class struggles and the spirit of resistance among the peasants there. Tzuchingshan was an extensive area of poor, mountain land, where people lived in dire poverty and most of them, besides tilling the land, eked out a living by gathering faggots and making charcoal. Feng Yun-shan had come to a village in this area to do revolutionary work in 1844. He earned his living by working and teaching, and

---

* C.A. Montalto de Jesus: *Historic Shanghai*, Shanghai, 1909, p. 119.

lived amongst the poor for three years. At night he would cross rugged mountains to other villages to propagate the doctrines of the Pai Shang Ti Hui. He inspired and organized people with a steady determination, and so gained more and more adherents.

Hung Hsiu-chuan went to Tzuchingshan in August 1847 when peasant uprisings were stirring in Kwangsi. The Pai Shang Ti Hui had already developed into a revolutionary organization with 2,000 to 3,000 followers in Hsiangchow, Hsunchow, Yuchow, Pingnan, Wuhsuan, Kueihsien, Popai and other places. Hung Hsiu-chuan was very pleased to see the revolutionary stronghold Feng Yun-shan had worked so hard to build up, and as he had long been highly commended by Feng Yun-shan, he was well received by the followers there, who put themselves under his orders and addressed him "Teacher Hung." From then on, as a result of their joint efforts, the popularity of the Pai Shang Ti Hui increased and the pace of revolution quickened. Members went to remote villages propagating their ideas and getting people to tear down temples and destroy idols.

Hung Hsiu-chuan learned of a temple to "King Kan" in Hsiangchow which the local people were very much afraid of, because the idol was said to have supernatural powers. In order to smash this superstitious belief, he and Feng Yun-shan led the people to the temple, struck the idol with a stout bamboo pole and enumerated its 10 crimes. After that they demolished the idol.

The news of this event spread far and wide and had a great impact. Not only was a "King Kan" destroyed, but the chain of feudalism was broken, and the people gained in confidence.

The struggle between the revolutionary Pai Shang Ti Hui and local reactionary forces intensified. A landlord at Wuhsuan who hated the Pai Shang Ti Hui organized a local armed force against it. In the winter of 1847, this landlord arrested Feng Yun-shan. The people soon rescued him. But the landlord persisted, arresting Feng again early in 1848 and charging him in the Kueiping magistrate's court with "blasphemy," "deceiving people with heretical beliefs," "unlawful assembly," and so on. This time Feng was put in jail. His imprisonment was a big setback for the preparation of the revolution. Hung Hsiu-chuan who was visiting relatives at Tzuku Village in Kueihsien when he heard of it hastened to Tzuchingshan and from there on to Canton to seek help to save Feng Yun-shan. Thus the Pai Shang Ti Hui was quite suddenly deprived of both its leaders. At this critical moment a man called Yang Hsiu-ching appeared, claiming to be the "Heavenly Father" descended to earth. He began preaching to the masses and reassured them. Shortly afterwards, a new figure, Hsiao Chao-kuei, appeared, claiming to be the "Heavenly Brother" come to earth. According to the Society's beliefs the "Heavenly Father" was the ultimate authority. Although by claiming the title Yang Hsiu-ching fulfilled the immediate need of the Pai Shang Ti Hui for a leader, his greed for power sowed the seeds of discord in the later Taiping Heavenly Kingdom. Yang, a native of Kueiping in Kwangsi, was from a poor family. Having been a charcoal burner and a tiller of hillside plots, and having worked as a porter on the wharves, he had little book-learning but was a good organizer. Hsiao Chao-kuei, born into a poor peasant family in Wuhsuan, Kwangsi, had a steady, courageous character. Thanks to the efforts of these two men, the Pai Shang Ti Hui flourished, and the charcoal makers of Tzuching-shan managed to collect enough to bribe the Hsunchow prefect and the Kueiping magistrate to release Feng Yun-shan. Thus the attempt of the landlord class to undermine the Pai Shang Ti Hui by arresting Feng Yun-shan backfired badly and actually strengthened the revolutionary forces.

With Hung Hsiu-chuan at their head, a group of leaders including Feng Yun-shan, Yang Hsiu-ching, Hsiao Chao-kuei, Wei Chang-hui and Shih

Ta-kai emerged from the revolutionary ranks of the Pai Shang Ti Hui. Wei Chang-hui, from Kueiping County in Kwangsi Province, was a landlord with more than 240 *mu* of land who infiltrated into the revolutionary ranks simply because he nursed a grudge against another landlord in his village. Shih Ta-kai, of Kueihsien County, was of landlord extraction but as a Hakka settler he had been discriminated against by the local landlords and unable to find any other sort of opening, he also joined the Pai Shang Ti Hui.

Once this leading group was formed, people were trained to fight and to make weapons. By 1850 the Pai Shang Ti Hui was growing fast; with Tzuchingshan as its base, it reached west to Wuhsuan, southwest to Kueihsien, east to Pingnan and Tenghsien, north to Hsiangchow, and south to Popai, Luchuan and Hsinyi in Kwangtung Province. Members could be found in almost every village. The majority were peasants, but there were a number of charcoal burners, miners, porters and handicraft workers among them. Destitute landless peasants with their great revolutionary spirit formed the mainstay of the revolution.

After a long period of preparation and mobilization, the time was ripe for revolution.

From the Chintien Uprising to the Establishment of the Heavenly Capital

3

In June and July 1850, on Hung Hsiu-chuan's orders, over 10,000 members of the Pai Shang Ti Hui began to gather in Chintien Village in the foothills of Tzuchingshan. As soon as they had assembled, they contributed what little they owned to the "Sacred Treasury," by which they were subsequently supported. They shared their food, clothing and money, an arrangement which suited their economic situation and their combatant life. Meanwhile, armed units were organized, and weapons, banners, clothes and bedding were distributed among them. Separate camps were set up for men and women soldiers, and strict military training was given. Thus a strong combat unit of the Taiping Army came into being.

On January 11, 1851, Hung Hsiu-chuan, Feng Yun-shan, Yang Hsiu-ching, Hsiao Chao-kuei, Wei

Chang-hui, Shih Ta-kai and others led the whole army at a grand ceremony in Chintien Village, where Hung Hsiu-chuan solemnly proclaimed the uprising and announced the establishment of the "Taiping Tien Kuo" (the Taiping Heavenly Kingdom). He also promulgated a simple military code with five rules:

1. Obey decrees and orders (including the Heavenly laws and commands).
2. Separate men's and women's regiments (men and women should be in separate camps).
3. Forbid the slightest violation of the people's interests.
4. Be selfless and friendly and obey chiefs.
5. Be co-operative and never retreat in battle.

The revolutionary Taiping Army marched out of Chintien Village in mighty columns and won their first victory by the capture of Chiangkouhsu, a major town on the Tahuang River.

After the rise of the Pai Shang Ti Hui in southern China, Hung Ta-chuan, leader of the Tien Ti Hui, offered to co-operate with Hung Hsiu-chuan. Hung Ta-chuan, or Chiao Liang as he was originally called, was a man of learning from Hunan. He nourished great revolutionary ambitions and had travelled around Hunan, Kwangtung and Kwangsi for many years, making numerous contacts with secret societies. The ranks of the Taipings were also swelled by many who had taken part in risings such as those led by Lo Ta-kang and Su San-niang. As the Tien Ti Hui had different beliefs from those of the Pai Shang Ti Hui, and was less strict in organization and discipline, some of its leaders soon broke away. However, Lo Ta-kang and Su San-niang retained their faith in the Taiping cause, and Lo, having won distinction in battle many times, became a prominent Taiping general.

The Ching government, very much alarmed by this flare-up in Kwangsi Province, immediately sent civil and military officials to deal with it. Hsiang Jung was made the Provincial Military Commander of Kwangsi, Chou Tien-chueh the Provincial Governor, and Li Hsing-yuan the Imperial Commissioner. Troops were transferred from Hunan, Kweichow, Yunnan and other provinces to encircle the Taiping Army and soon afterwards, the Grand Secretary Saishanga, the Deputy Military Governor Wulantai and various others were rushed to Kwangsi to direct military activity. Far from being held back by these forces, the Taipings continued their victorious march from Chiang-kouhsu to Wuhsuan, Kueiping and Pingnan, scoring repeated victories against the Ching troops. On September 25, the Taiping vanguard under Lo Ta-kang captured Yungan, the first city to be occupied by the Taipings since the Chintien Uprising.

Hung Hsiu-chuan issued a military code instructing the soldiers to do everything for the public welfare without any selfish motive, and to surrender all war booty to the "Sacred Treasury." He also sent people to the countryside to proclaim that the Heavenly soldiers had entered the land to kill the monsters, that all the inhabitants might peacefully pursue their occupations and that anyone who volunteered to join the Taiping Army would be supplied with food and clothing. The Taipings struck hard at the power of the landlords in the city of Yungan: they confiscated their property and ordered them to contribute money and grain. If they met resistance, they organized the people to search the landlords' houses, carry away their grain and pigs. They also called on the peasants not to pay rent.

The rapid development of the revolutionary situation necessitated a political organization. Following the uprising, Hung Hsiu-chuan had become the Heavenly King. After the capture of Yungan, he made Yang Hsiu-ching the Eastern Prince, Hsiao Chao-kuei the Western Prince, Feng Yun-shan the Southern Prince, Wei Chang-hui the Northern Prince, and Shih Ta-kai the Prince Yi. The Eastern Prince was to superintend the other princes. Chin Jih-kang, Hu Yi-huang, Lo Ta-kang and other Taiping generals were also assigned to official posts according to a new system, which included posts and titles like ministers, commanders-in-chief, army commanders, division commanders, etc. Thus an organized revolutionary leadership was constituted.

The Taipings also proclaimed their "Heavenly Calendar" at Yungan. According to the "Heavenly Calendar" the odd months had 31 days, and the even, 30, making a total of 366 days in a year. Since the earth in fact takes only 365¼ days to revolve around the sun, the new calendar was slightly in error. Nevertheless, its subsequent implementation throughout the Taiping realms was of considerable political and ideological significance, because it abolished the old system of dating from the first year of the reign of the current emperor, and did away with such superstitious notions as "lucky" or "unlucky" days in the old calendar.

The Ching troops besieged Yungan from the north and south, and set up a blockade hoping to strangle the new-born political power of the Taipings in the city.

Early in April 1852, the Taipings broke out of the besieged city, advanced eastwards towards Kusuchung, defeated the Ching troops stationed there and swept through their camp. Meanwhile, the southern prong of the Ching army under Wulantai pursued the Taipings into Kusuchung and inflicted heavy losses on their rear guard. Hung Ta-chuan was captured, and being recognized as an important Taiping leader, was sent under escort to Peking to be executed.

Kusuchung was 10 kilometres from Yungan, and seven and a half kilometres on from Kusuchung was the craggy area of Lungliaoling, over which towered Tatung Mountain. The Taiping soldiers, made cautious by their recent defeat, concealed their main forces in Tatung Mountain. Wulantai, emboldened by victory, pursued them too closely and fell straight into an ambush. The concealed soldiers rushed out, sword in hand, from both sides of the road. It was rainy and misty, and the narrow road was deep in mud. The Ching troops, unable either to advance or retreat, were thrown into confusion and suffered heavy casualties. Many of the Ching soldiers, including four generals, were killed. Wulantai lost his balance in the fighting and tumbled down the craggy hillside. Hsiang Jung pulled his troops back within the walls of Kweilin, while the Taipings continued their victorious advance on that city. Wulantai mustered the remnants of his troops in a last-ditch stand at Chiangchun Bridge outside the south gate of the city, but was mortally wounded by a cannon ball. Before his death, he memorialized the throne regretfully that he was not good at commanding troops.

The Taiping Army, having failed in an attempt to capture Kweilin by a surprise attack, abandoned their siege and turned northwards. Feng Yun-shan, the Southern Prince, was wounded by a cannon ball outside Chuanchow in northern Kwangsi. The Taipings captured Chuanchow on June 3, and were severe in their treatment of the Ching troops and their officers. Two days later, they withdrew from the city and following their original plan, marched on towards Hunan. They had got no further than Suoyitu, a ferry-point facing dangerous rapids not far from Chuanchow on the main route from that city to southern Hunan, when they were attacked by Ching troops who had been lying in ambush. Feng Yun-shan died from his wounds and the Taiping Army thus lost a brilliant leader.

The Ching troops failed to check the advance of the Taiping Army. On June 12, two days after the Suoyitu Battle, the Taipings captured Taochow in southern Hunan and began to reorganize their ranks. The Taiping Army issued three manifestos in the names of the Eastern Prince, Yang Hsiu-ching, and the Western Prince, Hsiao Chao-kuei, calling upon the people to rise up in revolt against the dark rule of the Ching dynasty. The following are some important points of the three manifestos:

1. The Taiping Army carries out the orders of Heaven.

2. Buddhist idols, the Monster King of Hell, and all the Ching rulers are alike; they are devils, the enemies of the people. The people must take up arms and slay the devils on behalf of Heaven.

3. The Ching government has committed hideous crimes. The world is ruled by greedy officials who exploit the people cruelly. Position can be bought and punishments commuted by bribery. The rich are in power, the heroes have no hope. If all the bamboo of the southern hills were to be used as paper, there would not be enough to detail their obscenities; if all the waves of the Eastern Sea were to be employed, they would not be sufficient to wash away their sins, which tower up to Heaven.

4. We give notice to all the armed forces of the landlords; the time has come for them to awake; and we hope that heroes and fighters will rise and hoist revolutionary banners in every province. The Tien Ti Hui and the Taipings, united in head and heart, will work together to exterminate the Ching dynasty.

In spite of their religious colouring, there is a strong spirit of political realism in these three manifestos. Poignantly written, with a clear-cut view on what to love and what to hate, they forthrightly expose and repudiate the evils of the feudal system, and of the Ching ruling class. Hundreds of thousands of people were roused to action by them on the long road taken by the Taipings from Hunan to Nanking.

The Taipings halted at Taochow for two months before taking Chenchow on August 17, where they burned down the Confucian Temple with its tablets to Confucius. The Taiping Army gained revolutionary fame and its strength was brought to almost 100,000, including the old members from Kwangsi. Among those who joined up in the region of Taochow and Chenchow were coal miners who later formed a unit which specialized in digging tunnels and blowing up city walls.

After the capture of Chenchow, the Taipings advanced rapidly on Changsha, the provincial capital of Hunan, launching their attack as soon as they arrived on its outskirts on September 11. Hsiao Chao-kuei was riding at the head of his troops waving them on with his sword when he was hit by a cannon ball and died. The Taipings, having fought vainly to capture Changsha for two months, switched their attack to Yochow, which they took in November. Soon afterwards, they captured Hanyang in Hupeh and began to build a floating bridge across the Yangtze from Hanyang to Wuchang, their next objective. At daybreak on January 12, 1853, they blew up the city wall with land mines. Eight standard-bearers then led the way over the walls, and the troops streamed into the city after them. In Wuchang the Taipings set up a "Sacred Treasury," "Men's Camps," "Women's Camps," and a clinic where the sick could be treated by doctors. Grain and salt were distributed daily. They ordered landlords and officials to contribute their gold and silver to the Taiping Heavenly Kingdom and they propagated their revolutionary ideas in the city to recruit more people for the revolution.

The capture of Wuchang, the first provincial city to be taken by the Taipings, had a great impact. The Hsien Feng Emperor, the overlord of the whole landlord class, was on pins and needles and complained that he could no longer eat or sleep in peace. To check the victorious advance of the Taipings, he appointed Lu Chien-ying, Viceroy of the Liangkiang Provinces (Kiangsu, Kiangsi and Anhwei) as an Imperial Commissioner and sent troops under his command to protect Kiangsu and Anhwei from the Heavenly Army.

In February 1853, under the general command of Hung Hsiu-chuan, the great army, now numbering 500,000, began an eastward advance, on land and water. The land forces under Hu Yi-huang, Li Kai-fang and Lin Feng-hsiang marched down both banks of the Yangtze while the navy, under Chin Jih-kang, Lo Ta-kang and Lai Han-ying sailed down the river itself. The sails of the boats blended into the army banners so that they formed a solid column of considerable width which stretched back for miles. They put Lu Chien-ying's forces stationed in Kuangchi County on the Yangtze in east Hupeh to flight. Lu himself took refuge in Nanking. The Taipings then captured Kiukiang, a spring-board to the provinces of Anhwei, Kiangsi and Hupeh, and also took Anking in Anhwei, another important strategic gain. Their tremendous success continued. On February 26, they captured Chihchow (present-day Kueichih in Anhwei), on March 4, Wuhu, and by March 8, they stood at the very gates of Nanking. The terror-stricken Ching government ordered that Lu Chien-ying be punished, but permitted him to make up for his defeat by meritorious services, in the hope that this would raise morale. However, the revo-lutionary forces remained invincible. On March 19, the Taipings mined the Yifeng Gate of Nan-king, breached the city wall and killed Lu Chien-ying. The next day, the Taiping soldiers made a triumphant and dignified entry into Nanking, 25 to a column, practically dressed, their heads covered with red scarves, and swords or spears in their hands. On entering the city, they conducted a search for officials who had concealed themselves. Then they proclaimed that "everyone must respect the Heavenly Father, obey the Heavenly King, struggle together to conquer the country and share the Heavenly happiness."

On March 29, followed and welcomed by more than 100,000 people, Hung Hsiu-chuan entered the city. Nanking was renamed "Tienching," the Heavenly Capital, and the former residence of the Viceroy of the Liangkiang Provinces became the Palace of the Heavenly King. Thus a peasant state power was established in opposition to the landlord power which the Ching dynasty represented.

Marx said: **"With the thoroughness of the historical action the size of the mass whose action it is will therefore increase."*** At the time of the Chintien Uprising, the Taiping Army had numbered only 10,000, on the march from Kwangsi to Nanking, it had grown to 1,000,000. The Taipings went from victory to victory because their revolution reflected the wishes of the people. No force on earth could hold back a movement so much in tune with popular feeling and general trends.

The Taiping Heavenly Kingdom created a com-

---

* Karl Marx and Frederick Engels: *The Holy Family.*

pletely new system of military organization. *Chun* (army) was used of a unit of the 13,125 combat troops under an army commander. In each army there were five *shih* (divisions), the forward, rear, left, right and centre, each containing 2,625 soldiers under a divisional commander. Under the division were *lu* (brigades), *tsu* (companies) and *liang* (platoons). Each platoon was made up of 25 soldiers divided into five squads. The command system was efficient, morale was high, and the Taiping Army must have made a magnificent picture, with bugles blowing and a forest of spears raised high. The troops had a common revolutionary aim and a real will to fight so they were greatly feared by the enemy.

Groups of handicraft workers were organized to supply military needs. Most of the women were in direct combat posts, but those who were unable to fight were organized in Women's Camps and were responsible for logistics. Old people made bamboo spikes to be planted in ditches and on the battlefields to keep out the enemy, cooked meals or did other such work. Children belonged to the Children's Guard, and helped adults in battle, showing great courage and intelligence. Everyone in the revolutionary ranks had their role to play, and all the work was attuned to the needs of the war. Thus a complete, flexible combat collective was formed.

Under this tight organization, Taiping discipline was very strict. Even in battle, regulations were often proclaimed, emphasizing such matters as military obedience, care of civilians, protection of weapons, the surrender to public ownership of all war booty and so on. This assisted the rapid growth in the strength of the Taipings.

Their growth inspired peasant uprisings in various places. Uprisings were organized by the Hsiao Tao Hui (Small Sword Society) in Fukien and Shanghai, by the Tien Ti Hui in Kwangtung and Kwangsi and by the Nien in Anhwei and Honan. The reactionary Ching rulers became panic-stricken at the extent of their influence, because as soon as they pacified one area, they lost hold of another.

The Taiping Revolution combined with these other forces of resistance to form a revolutionary high tide which swept across the whole country.

Karl Marx, the revolutionary leader of the proletariat, was watching the development of the Taiping Revolution with interest. In 1853 he wrote his famous essay "Revolution in China and in Europe" which contains high praise for the revolutionary movement then under way in China. Marx sympathized with what he described as **"the** chronic rebellions subsisting in China for about ten years past, and now gathered together in one formidable revolution,"* and evaluated it very highly. Thus, even at this time the Taiping Revolution had already made a strong impression throughout the world.

* Karl Marx: "Revolution in China and in Europe."

Measures Adopted After the Establishment of the Capital

After the establishment of the Heavenly Capital, the Taipings worked hard in the military, political and economic spheres to safeguard their capital and win further victories. As they prepared the defence of the city, the Taiping leaders began to extend, both inside and outside the city, the system which had been practised within their army since the Chintien Uprising. The military rule that men and women should be segregated was strictly observed. Most of the men who were fit went into the army, while the rest were sent to workshops or took up other types of productive employment on the basis of their former professions or skills and the needs of the moment. Old men, or those who were not very strong, did light jobs within their capacities, such as street-cleaning and keeping the night watch. All the women were organized in Women's Camps, except those most skilled at embroidery, who were recruited for specialist workshops. These women's embroidery workshops, like the other camp workshops, were responsible for specialized production under government management. These camps were also known as women's houses, for unlike women in the army, their members mainly undertook such ordinary jobs as helping with the harvest, transporting salt and grain, digging trenches, fashioning bamboo spikes and so on.

The "Sacred Treasury" system, which had been set up early in the Taiping Uprising, both encouraged strict military discipline and enabled the army to procure supplies very effectively. In the Heavenly Capital, this system was expanded, not only were all levies and war booty to go to the "Sacred Treasury," it was also laid down that the capital of all the merchants, since it belonged to the Heavenly Father, should be contributed to the "Sacred Treasury." Subsequently, all houses, precious metals, grain, merchandise and so forth were turned over to public ownership, valuables going to the "Sacred Treasury," while daily necessities were stored in various warehouses managed by the treasurers.

As to supplies, it was decided that no one, from the Heavenly King down to the ordinary soldiers should receive wages, although there was a difference in the meat ration. No one, soldier or civilian, was allowed to own private property and the needs of all were supplied from the public purse. People's clothing and food were provided by a public treasury to which all their wealth and properties went. They were well dressed and had more than enough grain to eat. But, later on, the system of the "Sacred Treasury" was undermined since, in fact, this kind of absolute equalitarianism is hard to maintain in the long run.

The Taipings adopted a system of centralized management of the various handicraft industries. Camps were set up to bring the handicraft workers of each trade with their raw materials together to work in specialized workshops, and officials were appointed to take charge of them. This was a most original measure for that period. Even the Taipings' enemies had to admit that within the Heavenly Kingdom trades were well organized to supply all the needs of the army promptly. But, since all trades and enterprises were centrally controlled, and their products mainly consumed by the army, they were isolated from the market forces of supply and demand which ultimately discouraged the producers and hindered the development of productive capacity.

At one point, the Taipings attempted to abolish commerce, saying: "Everything is granted by the Heavenly Father. It is not necessary to purchase things with money." In the circumstances this was not realistic, so they soon abandoned the prohibition in favour of a commercial system managed by the government, which, however, also failed within a few months. Outside the capital a free market was permitted, so soldiers from the city used to go out of it when they needed to buy something. In other districts under Taiping jurisdiction, merchants had simply to buy a license in order to be permitted to carry on business as usual at a low rate of tax, so that many cities and towns were crowded with merchants offering a variety of goods for sale.

The military, political and economic measures executed by the Taipings were intended to form the basis for their ideal "Heavenly Kingdom" on earth. In the winter of 1853, they issued their programme for social reform: the *Heavenly Land System*. A product of the age-old anti-feudal struggle of the peasants, this system utterly negated feudalism. It contained two measures of paramount importance. Firstly, it abolished the feudal landlord system, made the land public property and distributed it to the peasants to till, and secondly, it laid out a new basis for state power, the

"System of Local Officials," by means of which a new social structure could be set up to replace the old.

The *Heavenly Land System* ruled that all the land under Heaven should be cultivated by all the people under Heaven. If the people of one area ran short of land they might move elsewhere. Under Heaven rich harvests and poor harvests should be made to compensate for each other. Wherever the harvest was poor, people might obtain relief from places with rich harvests. Its ideal was that land, food, clothing and money should all be shared equally, and that all under Heaven should be well fed and well clad. In accordance with this principle, the document ruled that land should be divided into nine grades depending on yields at the two annual harvests, and distributed evenly among the people. A mixture of land of the nine grades was to be distributed to every family in conformity with the number of its members, regardless of sex. Half a share was allowed for those under the age of 16.

It was the economy of handicraft and small-scale peasant producers which gave birth to the stipulation in the *Heavenly Land System* that land distribution should be based on absolute equality. "The same livelihood for all," was advocated. After the distribution of land, each peasant household was to exist within a self-supplying small-scale economy based on a few *mu* of land, some mulberry trees, five hens, two pigs and so on. The surplus left from the annual harvests, once the everyday needs of the peasants had been satisfied, was to go to the public treasury, and would be used to pay for weddings and other such occasions. It was held that with this dispersed small-scale economy, the peasants would preserve equal shares of property forever. This dream reflected the peasants' longing for an ideal society without exploitation or poverty, where there would be no inequality, no hunger, and no lack of warm clothes. It was a fantasy which could never be realized. As Chairman Mao has pointed out: **"We support the peasants' demand for equal distribution of land in order to help arouse the broad masses of peasants speedily to abolish the system of landownership by the feudal landlord class, but we do not advocate absolute equalitarianism. Whoever advocates absolute equalitarianism is wrong."*** New productive forces and new relations of production were absent in the period of the Taiping Revolution, nor did new class forces or an advanced political party emerge. Naturally with the subjective desire of the peasants as its starting point, this land

---

* Mao Tsetung: Vol. IV, pp. 235-236.

programme was profoundly coloured with absolute equalitarianism.

As the Taipings proclaimed that all the land and wealth belonged to the "Emperor God," they regarded it as their common property. The regulation that land should be distributed evenly to everyone was intended to dispossess the feudal landlords and restore land to the peasants, thus extricating them from feudal exploitation. It reflected the general demand of the peasants for land, and was in fact, an advocacy of "land to the tillers." It was undeniably revolutionary in its opposition to the feudal system of landownership. Indeed, at that time, with Chinese capitalism about to appear, and under a strong stimulus from foreign capitalism, whatever the subjective desire of the Taiping leaders, objectively the Taiping Revolution was bound to pave the way for the development of capitalism. The formulations of the *Heavenly Land System* reflected this general historical trend.

This land programme, due perhaps to the exigencies of war or to the difficulties of implementation, was never carried out and was not even mentioned in later documents. But in the actual struggles of the Taipings, partly because of the anti-feudal nature of peasant war, and partly because of what the land programme made possible, the feudal system of landownership was shaken

48

to its very core. Among the orders carried out under the *Heavenly Land System* were:

1. The severe punishment of Ching officials or "monsters" as they were dubbed, of all ranks. Leaders of landlords' armed gangs who resisted were particularly firmly suppressed. Not only was feudal political power partly destroyed by these measures, large numbers of landlords fled to Shanghai and elsewhere and their great holdings of land, together with those of the temples which were destroyed, fell into the hands of the peasants. Consequently, in Yangchow for example, it was said that for three years, people had paid no rent, only contributions to the Taipings. So the Taiping Revolution brought a great increase in the number of cultivators who owned their own land in the lower Yangtze area.

2. In some villages around the Heavenly Capital, the tenants ceased to pay rent to the landlord, but they paid land tax on it to the revolutionary government thus confirming them in their possession of the land they had once rented. In other places, after the Taiping local official granted a "land certificate" to the tenants the landlords were forbidden to collect rents, which effectively negated their ownership in law. The landlords could not hide their greed when they saw the rich harvests, and sighed that they could get nothing

from the leased land. Although these things only occurred in certain places, they had the greatest significance for the transformation of the feudal system of landownership.

3. A rent reduction of 50 per cent was enforced in many places; some tenants paid only 2-3 pecks or 4-5 pecks per *mu*. Some landlords managed to collect a little rent from those tenants who were willing to pay, but could get nothing at all from those who refused, and many peasants demanded that their landlords hand a large part of the already reduced rent they collected over to the Taipings as land tax and other levies. The landlord class was also weakened by decrees ordering that they should surrender grain, precious metals, or other movable property.

Another important aspect of the *Heavenly Land System* was the "System of Local Officials." Under this system, local political administration was based on the Taiping military structure. The *chun* (army) leaders, *shih* (division) leaders, and so on down to the *liang* (platoon) leaders functioned as local officials. There were 13,156 families under an "army" leader, each of which was supposed to supply one soldier. In every "army" unit, there were offices in charge of land distribution, the criminal court, cash and grain, revenue, and expenditures, each headed by an official and his deputy. The basic unit, the "platoon" of 25 families, was approximately the size of a village. Each "platoon" had a public treasury from which both the costs of weddings and other such occasions, and of relief to orphans and the sick, disabled, childless or widowed were paid at fixed rates. Each "platoon" had a hall for worship where religious instruction was given and children were educated. Law suits, punishments and awards were also administered at this basic level and the "platoon" leaders reported on them to their immediate superiors. Thus a design was formed for a closely-integrated ideal society.

Although this design was not fully realized, a system in which political administration was based on the local official was put into effect. After the Taipings had set up their Heavenly Capital, whenever they captured new territory, they would give orders that a list of all the households in the prefecture or the county should be drawn up. Each district was then to recommend its own leaders below the "army" level, to take charge of such duties as tax collection and political instruction. This method of selecting local officials shows a real spirit of democracy. The authority immediately above the "army" was the *hsien,* or county, under an officer called *chienchun* (army supervisor), and above that came the *tsun* as the old prefecture was renamed, supervised by a *tsungchih*, an officer known as "the Preserver of the Land."

In accordance with the theory, "Under Heaven, all men are brothers and all women are sisters," the Taiping leaders insisted on the equality between men and women. In this context two important regulations of the *Heavenly Land System*, should be considered. The first, already mentioned, was that land was to be distributed to families on the basis of the number of their members, regardless of sex, indicating that women were to have economic equality with men. The second regulation, "Under Heaven marriage should have nothing to do with property," implied the abolition of the feudal institution of marriage by purchase. The Taipings respected women and accorded them equality with men as can be seen from the fact that there were women soldiers and women officials, and that many types of productive work were performed by women in their workshops. A British missionary (W. Muirhead) visiting the Heavenly Capital wrote: "While walking along the streets, the number of females that are seen on the way is rather a novelty. They are in general well dressed, and of very respectable appearance. Many are riding on horseback, others are walking, and most of them have large feet. Not a few stop to hear our preaching, and always conduct themselves with perfect propriety. This is new, as compared with the former course of things, and the whole reminds one partly of home life."* Obviously, the emancipation of women was an extremely important part of the anti-feudal programme of the Taipings.

---

* Quoted by Lin-le (Augustus F. Lindley) in *Ti-Ping Tien-Kwoh; The History of the Ti-Ping Revolution,* London, 1866, p. 472.

The Northern and Western Expeditions   5

After the occupation of Nanking, the victorious
Taiping Army captured two more towns in
Kiangsu Province, the most important strategically
in the lower Yangtze area — Chenkiang on the
southern bank and Yangchow a little to the north
of the river. Before taking Nanking, the Taipings
had failed to build up stable base areas in the
places which they had captured, so many of these
fell into the hands of the enemy again. Hence, their
bitter enemy Hsiang Jung was able to pursue them
from Kwangsi all the way to Nanking. Soon after
the Taipings established their Heavenly Capital at
Nanking, Hsiang Jung, by now an Imperial Commissioner, stationed his troops just to the east of it
at Hsiaolingwei. His camp there was known as
the "Great Camp South of the Yangtze." Meanwhile, Chishan, another Imperial Commissioner

54

sent by the Ching government, stationed his troops outside Yangchow and set up the "Great Camp North of the Yangtze." These camps were a constant threat to the Heavenly Capital. At this stage, however, the Taiping Army was still fighting well, and going from strength to strength. While defending their Heavenly Capital strongly, the Taiping leaders also drew up military plans for a northern expedition to take Peking and a western one to occupy Anhwei, Kiangsi and other provinces.

In May 1853, the Taipings sent out their northern expedition resolving to smash the Ching stronghold. Before the army left, Hung Hsiu-chuan ordered that its objective should be to drive rapidly through to Peking, taking advantage of weaknesses in the enemy lines, without losing time by trying to capture cities or seize territory. Under the command of two brave generals Li Kai-fang and Lin Feng-hsiang, about 20,000 picked men set out from Yangchow and broke through Linhuai-kuan into Anhwei, where they captured such cities as Fengyang, Huaiyuan and Mengcheng. Another Taiping force then marched into Anhwei under Chi Wen-yuan and Chu Hsi-kun joining forces with Li Kai-fang and Lin Feng-hsiang in the Pohsien County area for a joint march into Honan. This was the area in which the Nien, another great peasant rebellion of the 19th century, was most active. The Nien army and the Taiping expedition co-ordinated their operations, so that the Ching forces were unable to conduct an offensive in one place without losing territory elsewhere, and thus suffered repeated defeats. The ranks of the expeditionary force were swelled by many new recruits.

The northern expedition army crossed the Yellow River in Honan, and traversed a part of southern Shansi before driving northwards through Chihli Province (present-day Hopei). The Taiping vanguard neared Paoting in Chihli to the great alarm of the Peking government. Terrified, the Hsien Feng Emperor sent out a strong force to check its advance. Patrols were started in Peking and martial law was declared. The emperor prepared to take refuge in the old summer palace in Jehol. Over 30,000 officials and landlords fled from Peking.

With the way ahead blocked by an ever-increasing Ching force, the Taipings decided a direct advance was too difficult, and from Hsienhsien they marched southeast, passing through Chiaoho and Potou before veering north again, attacking Tsangchow and Chinghsien, and at the end of October, launching an offensive towards Tientsin. At this point, they were about 100 kilometres from

Peking. This was the most distant battlefield that the northern expedition was to reach. By now Tientsin was well guarded and the Ching troops who had pursued the Taiping Army were drawing near. The Taipings held out at Tuliu and Chinghai with desperate courage. Badly outnumbered, short of food and without winter clothing they encountered terrible hardships. In February 1854, they retreated southward, falling back in March on Fucheng and in early May on Lienchen, to wait for reinforcements from the Heavenly Capital. The relief troops actually reached Linching in Shantung Province, but there they were driven back by a counter-attack. Li Kai-fang led a part of the expeditionary army south to meet the relief army, but was cut off in Shantung first at Kaotang and then at Fengkuantun in Chihping County by the Ching armies. The northern expedition army was now in a very difficult situation, split into two sections which were cut off from each other by blockades and without reinforcements. Lienchen and Fengkuantun were taken by Ching troops under the Mongol general Sengalintsin in 1855. Lin Feng-hsiang and Li Kai-fang were taken prisoner and, like all their captured officers and men, were brutally slaughtered.

The northern expedition army had driven through six provinces, carrying the struggle forward over 2,500 kilometres and causing the Ching government the gravest alarm. But the Taiping leaders made a grave strategic blunder in failing to launch an all-out action to topple the Ching government and destroy its power in the central plains for once and for all. They sent rather a small force on the northern expedition which became so isolated as it penetrated deep into enemy territory that relief forces were unable to get through to save it from defeat. Thus the Taipings lost an excellent chance to capture Peking and the Ching government gained a breathing space in which to secure its position, rally its forces and prepare a counter-attack.

When they dispatched the northern expedition, the Taipings also sent a force west up the Yangtze River. In May 1853, commanded by Hu Yi-huang, Lai Han-ying and Shih Chen-hsiang, a river navy of over 1,000 gunboats sailed for Anking, Kiukiang and Wuchang, three military strongholds which if taken would give the Taipings control of the upper Yangtze, make the Heavenly Capital safer, and by cutting the Ching communications with the area south of the Yangtze, would secure Taiping territory in that area.

The Taiping force pushed ahead rapidly taking Anking in June, Kiukiang in September, and then, still fresh from these victories, it captured Hankow and Hanyang. To back up their forces at Anking and control northern Anhwei, the Taipings then besieged Luchow (present-day Hofei) in December 1853, and captured the city in January 1854 together with a large area of Anhwei. In February 1854, the Taipings campaigned in Hupeh, gained control of Hanyang three times, and took Wuchang after a siege. In March they broke through into Hunan from several directions, taking Yochow, Hsiangyin and various other places. When they entered Hunan, however, they encountered a new enemy, bitterly opposed to them — Tseng Kuo-fan.

Tseng Kuo-fan, a vice-president of the Board of Rites, was a big landlord in Hsianghsiang in Hunan Province. In 1853, he was at home observing the customary mourning period following his mother's death. The Hsien Feng Emperor, conscious that the inferior Ching troops were everywhere losing to the Taipings, ordered the officials and landlords of the provinces north and south of the Yangtze to raise a militia to remedy the situation. Tseng Kuo-fan, an obdurate member of the landlord class and a defender of the feudal system, detested the Taipings. As soon as he was ordered to raise a militia in Hunan, he began to organize the notorious Hunan Army. The generals of this army, mostly, like Tseng himself, natives of the district of Hsianghsiang, were reactionary Confucian scholars who had sworn to brave death in the defence of the Ching dynasty and Confucian precepts. Tseng Kuo-fan exploited provincialism and feudal clan loyalty to ensure obedience in his army. Each regimental commander was supposed to recruit his own soldiers who were answerable only to him, while Tseng Kuo-fan was in personal command of them all. Thus a counter-revolutionary force was built up, bound by an intense feudal relationship. Tseng's militia began at once to put down the peasants in its area and within a few weeks more than 200 of them had been massacred. Angry voices were raised everywhere denouncing "Tseng the Head-Chopper." In March 1854 the Hunan Army, whose land and water forces together numbered 17,000 men, was formally constituted. It was the biggest landlord militia force of the time, and from it later emerged the first counter-revolutionary warlord clique in modern China.

After the formation of the Hunan Army, Tseng Kuo-fan wrote "A Call to Arms to Subjugate the Kwangtung Bandits," a nauseous counter-revolutionary essay which proclaimed his profound hatred of the revolution, lamenting that the landlords could not collect rent or taxes, that merchants could not continue their prosperous business, nor could the gentry "recite Confucian canons." He said: "All the proprieties, virtues, human relationships, classics and moral codes China has possessed for several thousand years are being discarded and swept away at one stroke. . . . Confucius and Mencius are weeping in the underworld. How can those who have some book-learning sit by with folded arms and do nothing about it?" In this way he tried to mobilize the landlords and intelligentsia against the Taiping Revolution.

In April 1854, preparing to move eastwards Tseng Kuo-fan led the Hunan Army against Yochow. The Taipings met them head on, drove them back on Changsha, and following up their victory, captured Chingkang to the north of Changsha, and Hsiangtan to the south, in preparation for an attack on the city from both directions. In order to clear the threat from the north, Tseng Kuo-fan led an attack on Chingkang on April 28. The Taipings began a heavy bombardment of the enemy boats, which made them circle around in desperation for they could get no further. A special squad had been detailed to cut the tow-ropes of the enemy boats and they were thus thrown into complete confusion. Meanwhile, on land the Hunan Army was also breaking under the Taiping onslaught. To arrest their flight, Tseng Kuo-fan had a standard erected which read: "Those who go past this banner will be executed." But having lost their morale, the Hunan troops would no longer observe discipline and they continued to flee, making a detour to pass the banner.

In the battle, the Hunan Army was almost completely demolished. Angry and humiliated, Tseng Kuo-fan tried to drown himself but was saved by his followers. The Taiping forces had entered Hunan in numbers too small for them to give a death-blow to the newly-organized counter-revolutionary forces and Tseng Kuo-fan, therefore, had a breathing space of three months in which he had his navy rebuilt, recruited more soldiers and prepared a counter-attack.

At the end of July that year, once more on the offensive, the Hunan Army occupied Yochow. In August, in a counter-attack a veteran Taiping general, Tseng Tien-yang, engaged the Hunan troops at Chenglingchi, routed several hundred of them, and destroyed more than 30 enemy boats. Then he faced Tachipu, the Military Commander of Hupeh and one of the fiercest of the Hunan generals, but now ready to retreat because fighting with Tseng Tien-yang, he was unable to play any of his tricks. Unfortunately, just at this time Tseng Tien-yang was hit in the chest by a stray bullet. Furious, he dashed forward with a loud cry, killing any enemies he could reach. He slashed at Tachipu but missed and struck only his horse. Tseng Tien-yang himself then fell from the saddle and died a hero's death.

In the face of these setbacks, the Taipings were forced to retreat from Hunan. The Hunan Army pursued them by three different routes, straight down the Yangtze to Kiukiang in Kiangsi. Tseng Kuo-fan raised the arrogant slogan: "Sweep the Yangtze region clean, drive directly on Nanking."

In this dangerous situation, under orders from Hung Hsiu-chuan to relieve the western forces, Shih Ta-kai, Hu Yi-huang and Lo Ta-kang led their troops to Poyang Lake in Kiangsi, where they won a great victory and frustrated the enemy's offensive.

When the Taipings arrived at the mouth of the lake, they practised a very flexible strategy, avoiding combat while they first strengthened their defences. Every night they harassed and frightened the soldiers of the enemy flotilla, sending out small craft to attack it with fire-balls, and scouts who operated along the banks of the Yangtze beating war-drums and shooting fire-arrows at the enemy boats. Late in January 1855, the Taipings withdrew the troops who were guarding the mouth of Poyang Lake and thus successfully lured in more than 100 enemy boats. They were then able to cut these off from the rest of their fleet still in the Yangtze, by blocking the entrance to the lake again. They bagan to pick off the enemy forces one by one, and destroyed 40 of the enemy boats anchored on the Yangtze. The defeated Hunan Army fled to Kiukiang. The Taiping forces under the command of Lo Ta-kang pursued them, and even captured Tseng Kuo-fan's flag-ship though Tseng himself escaped in a small boat. He attempted to drown himself once more but his underlings pulled him back, and they fled to Nanchang.

After the great victory of Poyang Lake, the Taipings launched a counter-attack, retaking Hanyang and Wuchang, and driving back into Kiangsi, where within a few months they had captured seven prefectures,* one sub-prefecture and more than 50 counties.** Nanchang, Kuang-hsin, Jaochow, Kanchow and Nanan were the only prefectures still in the hands of the Ching army. Tseng Kuo-fan, entrenched at Nanchang in northern Kiangsi, was deeply worried by the Taiping encirclement. He complained that he had asked for help to no avail and that he was unable to relax even when he slept.

---

* A prefecture (*fu*) was a sub-division of a province.
** The county (*hsien*) and the sub-prefecture (*chow*) were sub-divisions of a prefecture.

However, in the meantime, a dangerous situation had arisen on the outer perimeter of the Heavenly Capital forcing the Taipings to pull back from the western front in order to break the enemy stranglehold on the Heavenly Capital. Tseng Kuo-fan could breathe again.

Smashing the Camps North and South of the Yangtze

6

The Great Camps North and South of the Yangtze which had been set up immediately after the Taipings took Nanking were not, in spite of their proximity, able to harm the Heavenly Capital directly, yet they became a serious menace to its security, harrying the northern and western expeditions, making constant trouble on the outer perimeter of the city area, and carrying out all sorts of plots and sabotage.

The Ching government eventually stationed 17,000 men at the Great North Camp under the command of Chishan, the Imperial Commissioner who had betrayed the country and surrendered to the enemy in the Opium War. When the Taipings started out on their northern expedition from Yangchow, forces from the Great North Camp pursued and harassed them. The departure of the expedition left the defending forces at Yangchow under strength, and the Ching troops took the chance to lay siege to the city. Late in December 1853, a shortage of food forced the Taiping Army to evacuate Yangchow, but as it was followed by all the young, able-bodied men and women, the city which Chishan occupied was almost deserted. When he fell sick and died after holding Yangchow for more than a year, he was succeeded by Tominga, another Ching general. During this interval, troops from the Great North Camp pushed through to Yicheng, attacked Kuachow and in co-ordination with the Ching troops from the Great South Camp harassed Chenkiang and Pukow, giving the Taipings a great deal of trouble.

Meanwhile, 20,000 men, constituting the main Ching force sent against the Taiping capital, were stationed at the Great South Camp which was close to the walls of the Heavenly Capital. Hsiang Jung was the commander of this camp. Chang Kuoliang, the deputy commander, was an ex-member of the Tien Ti Hui who had betrayed it and deserted to the Ching government. Troops from this camp constantly harassed the Heavenly Capital. In co-operation with the troops of Chirhanga, the Provincial Governor of Kiangsu, they laid siege to Chenkiang, made constant raids in the area between it and the Heavenly Capital, and blockaded the Yangtze interrupting the transportation of supplies to the Taiping capital and to Chenkiang. The Taiping Army, therefore, decided to launch an operation to wipe them out.

They planned a counter-encirclement campaign against both the Ching camps, starting from Chenkiang, a buffer for the Heavenly Capital which lay below it on the Yangtze. In 1855 the city encircled by Ching troops had run short of food, and its commander, Wu Ju-hsiao, whose forces were inadequate, was waiting for reinforcements. In February 1856, Chin Jih-kang, the Prince Yen, was ordered to lead Chen Yu-cheng, Li Hsiu-cheng, Chou Sheng-kun and their troops down the Yangtze to relieve the hard-pressed city. They fought their way down to Chenkiang, destroying many Ching camps as they went. Hoping to launch a pincer attack against the enemy, they sent Chen Yu-cheng with a few of his braves on a perilous mission to try to sneak into the city. They came under heavy fire as they sailed down the Yangtze to Chenkiang in a light boat, but reached the city without mishap through its water gate, and at last made contact with Wu Ju-hsiao. On April 1, Chin Jih-kang led his great army in a dawn attack on the enemy's camp. Bitter fighting continued until noon. Wu Ju-hsiao and Chen Yu-cheng then led a sally out of the city. The Ching troops, under attack from two sides, collapsed, thus bringing an end to the siege of Chenkiang.

As soon as Chin Jih-kang reached Chenkiang, he ordered that vessels be prepared through the night to ferry the great army across the Yangtze from Kinshan. They arrived at Kuachow on the north bank of the Yangtze in the early morning on April 3, and moving on quickly towards Yangchow, they defeated Tominga at Tuchiao and then won battles at the Ching camps of Hungchiao, Poshuwan and Sanchaho. Over 120 encampments of the Great North Camp collapsed. After the Taipings retook Yangchow on April 5, food supplies could again pass from that city to Chenkiang. The Ching Emperor was very angry at this great setback to his troops north of the Yangtze and ordered that Tominga and some other generals be discharged and prosecuted. Tehsinga, a Deputy Provincial Military Governor, was appointed Imperial Commissioner to reassemble the dispersed troops in the area north of the Yangtze. Chin Jih-kang and Chen Yu-cheng launched an attack on Pukow from Yangchow, and in late May, they led their troops across the Yangtze from Kuachow to attack the Ching troops on the southern bank. At the beginning of June, they captured over 70 encampments around Chenkiang. Chirhanga died in this defeat, though it is not clear whether by his own hand or not.

Having won these victories in the north of the Yangtze and at Chenkiang, the Taiping Army began the annihilation campaign they had planned against the Great South Camp hard by the walls of their capital.

The Great South Camp commanded by Hsiang Jung was based on Hsiaolingwei with outlying encampments in the hills along the eastern edge of the Heavenly Capital and in the districts of the Chinhuai River, Shihchiu Lake and Kucheng Lake to the south of the city. The Taipings launched an offensive against them. Shih Ta-kai was ordered to lead his army of 30,000 back to the capital from Kiangsi by two routes. The army which took the southern route passed through Tangtu in Anhwei and, on June 13, they captured Lishui County, a buffer for the whole Soochow-Changchow area of Kiangsu. Hsiang Jung rushed picked troops to save Lishui, thus upsetting troop dispositions at the Great South Camp. On June 14, Chin Jih-kang and Li Hsiu-cheng returned to the capital from the Chenkiang battlefront. In obedience to an order from Yang Hsiu-ching, they moved camp to Yaohuamen and Hsienhemen, east of the capital, in order to attack the enemy from the rear. The north route army under Shih Ta-kai arrived at the capital on June 18, and after making dozens of encampments around Yaohuamen and Hsienhemen, joined forces with Chen Yu-cheng and advanced to Huangmachun, cutting the road between the Ching camp at Hsiaolingwei and Hsienhemen and Shihpuchiao. In the meantime, the south route army which had captured Lishui was also pressing steadily on. The Taiping noose was drawing tighter. In the early morning of June 20, the Taiping troops started to attack from several directions, and those stationed in the capital also sallied out by different gates. They fought bitterly for the whole day before the defeated Ching troops finally fled in confusion. As night drew on, fire-arrows began to flash into Hsiaolingwei. Soon it and all the other Ching encampments were burning. The Great Camp had collapsed. Some officers and men of the Ching army died, and others ran away. Chang Kuo-liang, Hsiang Jung's deputy, was wounded in his left leg. Hsiang Jung himself fled with the remnants of his army to Tanyang in Kiangsu where in August he died in deep depression, some say by his own hand. Chang Kuo-liang, bitterly hostile to the Taipings, kept on making trouble for them with the men he had left to him.

The collapse of the Great South Camp relieved the Taipings of the pressure the Ching troops had been able to exert on their capital for three years. To the delight of both troops and populace, large quantities of munitions and supplies could once more be brought into the city.

7

The Internal Strife in the Heavenly Capital

After three years of continuous struggle, the Taipings had won many great victories. By 1856 they controlled eastern Hupeh and most of Kiangsi and Anhwei, and by smashing the Great North and Great South Camps, had at last raised the siege of the Heavenly Capital. They were in fact at the zenith of their military power. From Wuhan to Chenkiang numerous boats moved busily up and down the Yangtze, which was a great artery linking and co-ordinating the various parts of the Taiping Heavenly Kingdom. Only one cloud darkened the Taiping horizon! The internal dissension which was so to harm the development of the revolution had begun in the Heavenly Capital.

This dissension arose from Yang Hsiu-ching's monopoly of political and military power, which played havoc with the leadership system. Yang

Hsiu-ching was proud of his achievements in combat, and since his arrival at Nanking, he had become arrogant and domineering. He often attacked Hung Hsiu-chuan in the name of Heavenly Father, and had even wanted to flog him. His reprehensible behaviour upset relations within the Taiping leadership.

Wei Chang-hui, a landlord who had wormed his way into the Taiping leadership, made use of this situation. He did all he could to flatter Yang Hsiuching. If he caught sight of Yang's sedan chair, he would rush out to welcome him. Once, Wei Chang-hui's elder brother was involved in a dispute with the brother of Yang Hsiu-ching's concubine over the possession of a house. To please Yang, who had ordered him to punish his brother, Wei Chang-hui prescribed the death penalty which was carried out by attaching the victim to five horses so that he was torn asunder when they were driven apart. After this execution he said that only in this way could the masses be warned. With this sycophancy Wei Chang-hui made an outward show of submission to Yang while secretly awaiting the chance to strip him of his power and position. Even Tseng Kuo-fan saw this for he wrote in an intelligence report: "Outwardly, Wei Changhui is all obedience to Yang Hsiu-ching, inwardly he intends to seize power."

In August 1856, Yang Hsiu-ching made a bid to enlarge his powers still further, taking all the credit for the defeat of the Great South Camp and the death of Hsiang Jung in order to strengthen his case. He tried to force Hung Hsiu-chuan to give him the title "Wan Sui" ("Ten Thousand Years"). Hung Hsiu-chuan found this intolerable. He promised Yang to invest him on his birthday, September 23, and having delayed things with this pretext, he called Wei Chang-hui, Shih Ta-kai and Chin Jih-kang back to the Heavenly Capital to deal with Yang Hsiu-ching.

Wei Chang-hui hastened back from Kiangsi to the Heavenly Capital with 3,000 men loyal to him. Arriving at night on September 1, he had Yang Hsiu-ching's palace surrounded immediately and blocked off all the roads which led to it. Just before dawn, he and his followers broke into the palace. Yang Hsiu-ching was stabbed to death and his relatives and his staff were all massacred. By the time the sun rose, bloody corpses lay in piles inside and outside the building. When Hung Hsiu-chuan reprimanded Wei Chang-hui for this indiscriminate slaughter, Wei craftily agreed to be flogged and tricked all Yang's former followers into coming to see him "punished." He then had them all disarmed, and another bloody massacre took place. Those who escaped were pursued for days afterwards and killed when they were caught. In the turmoil stirred up by Wei Chang-hui, over 20,000 fine Taiping officers and soldiers lost their lives in the space of two months.

When Shih Ta-kai who was then on active service in Wuchang heard this, he and some of his commanders immediately set out for the capital, where they arrived in the latter part of September. Having learned the details of what had happened from the Heavenly King, he condemned Wei for killing so many innocent people. Fearing that Shih Ta-kai might thwart his attempt to seize power, Wei then decided to kill him too. When Shih got to hear of this he slipped over the city wall by night near the southern gate. Wei Chang-hui surrounded the Prince Yi's palace that night, but Shih of course was nowhere to be found, so Wei sent soldiers to hunt for him and had all the members of his family put to death. Shih Ta-kai in his refuge of Ningkuo in Anhwei was filled with bitter rage and began to assemble a large army for a punitive expedition against Wei Chang-hui.

Wei Chang-hui's behaviour had long since incurred the anger of both troops and officers in the Heavenly Capital. At Hung Hsiu-chuan's order "all people must be united with one heart in the Heavenly Kingdom," they arrested Wei and his followers and put them to death. They took Wei

Chang-hui's head to Shih Ta-kai's camp at Ning-kuo as proof of what they had done, and asked him to come back to help the government in the capital. Since the root of the trouble had now been dealt with, the great massacres in the capital came to an end.

Of course, Yang Hsiu-ching was himself to blame for his death. But in memory of his contribution to the Taiping cause, Hung Hsiu-chuan afterwards named September 2, the day of his death, the East Ascension Festival, meaning that it was the day on which the Eastern Prince had ascended to Heaven, and appointed his only surviving son to succeed him.

In November 1856, when Shih Ta-kai returned to the capital, he was entrusted with the state affairs of the whole kingdom and also given high official rank by the Heavenly King. But he had come back secretly intending to take any chance to seize power. After the recent turmoil Hung Hsiu-chuan was still a little wary of Shih Ta-kai, so when he promoted him, he also named his own two elder brothers, Hung Jen-fa and Hung Jen-ta, the Prince An and the Prince Fu. When he realized that he was being controlled by these two princes who were both greedy and mean, Shih became disaffected with Hung Hsiu-chuan and in May 1857, he used the excuse that the Heavenly

King was "too suspicious and too jealous" to leave the capital and openly raised the banner of separatism.

As Shih Ta-kai was leaving, he posted bulletins along the roadside proclaiming his disaffection with Hung Hsiu-chuan. Thus he was able to trick some of their crack troops into joining his breakaway movement, which weakened the Taipings, aggravated the problems which had followed the internal dissensions and had a bad effect on the military situation.

Wuchang had fallen to the enemy after Shih Ta-kai and his men had returned to the capital, and the greater part of Kiangsi was also lost. In May 1858, the Hunan Army retook Kiukiang, which gave them access to Hupeh, Kiangsi and Anhwei, and then pressed on down the river to Anking. Meanwhile, the Ching troops had rebuilt the Great South Camp and the Great North Camp. In July 1857, troops from the Great South Camp under the Imperial Commissioner Hochun, retook Chujung and Lishui in Kiangsu, and in December Chenkiang also fell to them. In order to blockade the Taiping capital, the enemy dug huge trenches running from the Yangtze islet of Chianghsinchow in the west to Yentzuchi in the north. In December of the same year, troops from the Great North Camp under the Imperial Commissioner Tehsinga captured Kuachow, and then Pukow, and started a co-ordinated offensive with troops from the Great South Camp with Anking and the Heavenly Capital itself as their main targets.

The Ching government ordered Tseng Kuo-fan to check Shih Ta-kai and his force of 200,000 men who were wandering from one area to another in Kiangsi, Chekiang, Fukien and Hunan, but Tseng, an old hand at trickery and deception, sent only a small force under a lesser general out after Shih because he could see that his movements were aimless, so he no longer regarded him as a major protagonist.

Arriving in Kwangsi in 1860, Shih Ta-kai began to recruit new followers and change the whole system of the Taiping Heavenly Kingdom. This made many of the officers and soldiers whom he had tricked into following him suspicious, and they demanded to return to the Heavenly Capital. An army of 200,000 under the command of Peng Ta-shun, Chu Yi-tien and 60 other officers, left Shih Ta-kai to march the tremendous distance back to the capital. They fought their way through to Kwanghsin in Kiangsi, where at last, in September 1861, they joined forces with units of the main Taiping Army. Hung Hsiu-chuan was so pleased when he heard the news that he awarded the army the title of "The Heavenly Army defending the Heavenly Dynasty."

Meantime, Shih Ta-kai, though opposed by the masses and deserted by his followers, had not been forgotten by the Ching government. He left Kwangsi with an army of some tens of thousands hoping to take Szechuan and make himself king there. He entered Yunnan from Kweichow heading for Szechuan. In May 1863, he set out from Chaotung in Yunnan, crossed the Chinsha River and hurried on to cross the Tatu River, then on the border of Szechuan. But all his attempts to fight his way across the Tatu failed. In hopeless straits, he thought that if he made an abject surrender his life might be spared. So he wrote a letter to Lo Ping-chang, the Viceroy of Szechuan, praising that murderer as "renowned for faith" and humbly asking him to deliver the letter sueing for mercy to the Ching Emperor. On receiving his letter of submission, the Ching troops put up a banner at their camp at Hsimaku, proclaiming that those who submitted would be spared. On June 13, Shih Ta-kai and his son Shih Ting-chung went over to surrender. In the enemy camp, Shih Ta-kai wrote a "confession," pleading for his life, but the enemy showed no mercy, and he was executed.

The Ching troops took advantage of Wei Chang-
hui's treachery and Shih Ta-kai's break-away
movement to launch fierce attacks on the Taipings
at various points north and south of the Yangtze,
reoccupying many places and compelling the Taipings to abandon their earlier offensive tactics for
defensive ones. In 1858, Anking and the capital
itself, the heart of the Taiping Heavenly Kingdom,
were in great difficulties with the enemy at their
very gates. Tseng Kuo-fan and some of the other
leaders exulted that the Taiping Army was hard-
pressed and would not last out the year. This reflected the gravity of the situation. At this difficult time, Hung Hsiu-chuan promoted some
young generals who had given many years to the
Taiping struggle, Chen Yu-cheng, Li Shih-hsien
and Yang Fu-ching, to the leadership. Li Hsiu-

cheng was also promoted at this time. They adopted an active defence strategy, initiating attacks themselves and ensuring their own survival by launching attacks on the aggressive enemy.

Chen Yu-cheng was one of the most outstanding of the many great heroes steeled in the revolutionary struggle of the Taipings. He had joined the Taiping uprising when he was only 14, and like other members of the Children's Guard he followed the troops, charging through the enemy lines with them. He proved to be extremely able, and soon became an officer in the Children's Guard. He often accomplished difficult missions involving feats such as scaling precipitous mountains and swimming in perilous waters. He took any chance to launch surprise attacks, withdrawing with such speed that the enemy were left in confusion. He was later entrusted with regular military duties. In 1854, when Wuchang was under siege, he led 500 men round to the east side of Wuchang. Then he divided his forces, sending 300 men to feign an attack on the city while he himself led the other 200 to scale the city wall, waving banners and shouting, "The Heavenly soldiers are coming." The Ching troops guarding the city scattered immediately in fright, streaming away from the gates, and the Taiping Army captured Wuchang. In the spring of 1856, it was Chen Yu-cheng who broke through the enemy's heavy encirclement of Chen-kiang in a single light craft, again showing courage and ability. As the years went by, he always was to be found wherever the enemy was most numerous. Now, in this time of crisis for the Taipings, it fell to Chen Yu-cheng to assume the responsibilities of commander-in-chief on the battlefront.

In August 1858, Chen Yu-cheng and Li Hsiu-cheng called Li Shih-hsien, Huang Wen-chin and the senior officers of various armies to a military council at Tsungyang in northern Anhwei to consider how to lift the siege of the Heavenly Capital. They decided to launch a co-ordinated offensive. After the meeting, Chen Yu-cheng captured Luchow and pressed on to the market town of Wuyi in Chuchow (present-day Chuhsien), where he joined forces with another unit of the Taiping Army. On September 25, they defeated Tehsinga, the commander of the Great North Camp, and Shengpao, the Imperial Commissioner for military affairs of Anhwei Province, at Wuyi, wiping out over 4,000 of the enemy. The next day, they defeated a relief force sent from the Great South Camp near Kiangpu and followed up their victory with an assault on Pukow. Chen Yu-cheng engaged Tehsinga's front line while other detachments made a surprise attack on his rear, reinforced by the Taiping soldiers from Chiufuchow who swam forward to their aid. Under fire from two directions, over 10,000 men of the Great North Camp were annihilated and Kiangpu was captured. When the Taiping vanguard reached Yangchow early in October, Tehsinga abandoned the city to them and fled. In the course of the heavy fighting in and around Pukow which lasted more than a month, the Taipings once more smashed the Great North Camp, restored communication between their capital and the area north of the Yangtze and cleared the Ching blockade to the north of the Heavenly Capital.

The Taipings' next great victory was at the famous Battle of Sanho.

While the Taipings were engaged in the vital struggle with the Great North Camp, the Hunan Army left Taihu County in Anhwei, to march against Anking and Luchow by various routes. In October, Li Hsu-pin, a bellicose Hunan general, led a strong force from Chienshan, Tungcheng and Shucheng, which arrived at Sanho on the western bank of Chaohu Lake, 45 kilometres from Luchow, in early November. Sanho had not previously been fortified, but when the Taipings were campaigning in northern Anhwei, they built city walls round it and constructed nine bastions, turning Sanho into a stronghold where they stored rations and munitions in support of Luchow and the capital. When the Hunan Army got there, it captured all the bastions. On learning that Sanho was in danger, Chen Yu-cheng led his troops west, marching day and night from Luho and Kiangpu, passing Chaohu Lake and Lukiang County. On November 7, he reached Paishihshan and Chinniuling, hemming in Sanho from the rear to cut off Li Hsu-pin's line of retreat. He also ordered Wu Ju-hsiao, the garrison commander at Luchow, to cut off the troops coming to reinforce the enemy, which rapidly completed their encirclement.

On November 14, Chen Yu-cheng led a raid on Li Hsu-pin's headquarters. The next day at daybreak, the Hunan Army launched a counter-attack on Chinniuling. Chen Yu-cheng's forces outflanked the enemy to their left and took them by surprise from the rear. A heavy fog reduced visibility to less than one metre. Li Hsu-pin's men, hearing people approach but not knowing where they were, became panic-stricken. Meanwhile, the Taiping reinforcements which had just arrived at Paishihshan rushed into the fray, and Wu Tingkuei, the garrison commander at Sanho, also took the chance to break out. Together all these forces stormed the enemy military camps which, after bitter hand-to-hand combat, were entirely destroyed. Li Hsu-pin, the most indulged of the Hunan generals, and Tseng Kuo-fan's brother,

Tseng Kuo-hua, were killed while 6,000 officers and men under Li's command, considered the cream of the Hunan Army, were wiped out. This was a tremendous blow to the whole Hunan Army. In Hsianghsiang in Hunan, where it had originated, rites for the dead were to be heard almost everywhere. Greatly cast down, Tseng Kuo-fan and Hu Lin-yi worried that the Sanho defeat had seriously undermined morale and the crack troops who were the fruit of four years' labour had been annihilated in a day. Hu Lin-yi, a native of Yiyang, Hunan Province, and at this time Governor of Hupeh, next in power only to Tseng Kuo-fan in the Hunan Army, came to Tseng's aid with all the forces at his disposal.

In the victorious Sanho campaign, the Taipings retook Shucheng and Tungcheng, frustrating for a time the enemy plan to encircle Luchow and Anking. Taiping morale rose accordingly, their fighting spirit improved, and soon there were reports of victorious counter-attacks from many areas.

In April 1859, soon after the Sanho victory, Hung Jen-kan arrived in the Heavenly Capital from Hongkong. His arrival and the proposals for reform which he put to Hung Hsiu-chuan were milestones in the political history of the latter period of the Taiping Heavenly Kingdom.

Hung Jen-kan, a cousin of Hung Hsiu-chuan's, like him of peasant origin, had also been a village school master. He and Feng Yun-shan had been activists when Hung Hsiu-chuan was forming the Pai Shang Ti Hui in his native countryside. Although he had not taken part in the Pai Shang Ti Hui struggle in Kwangsi, he had retained contact with Hung Hsiu-chuan. After the Chintien Uprising, he went to Kwangsi in response to the Taiping call, but returned to Kwangtung as he was unable to catch up the Heavenly Army. In 1852, he went to Hongkong where he received instruction from the London Missionary Society and American Baptist Church. In 1854, Hung Jen-kan left Hongkong to try to get through to the Heavenly Capital from Shanghai, but this proved difficult as the Soochow-Changchow area was still under Ching control. He thought of joining the Small Sword Society then in revolt in Shanghai but its leader, suspicious of his relationship with Hung Hsiu-chuan, refused to accept him. He studied astronomy, mathematics and the calendar in the church-run "Mohai Academy," and when winter came, he returned to Hongkong by steamer. However, he had not forgotten the Taiping cause, and in 1858, he left Hongkong yet again for the north. Travelling through Kwangtung, Kiangsi and Hupeh, he disguised himself as a merchant or a doctor in order to escape the enemy's notice, and finally arrived in the following year at the Heavenly Capital, where the central leadership of the Taipings had still not recovered from the effects of internal dissension. Hung Hsiu-chuan was delighted by Hung Jen-kan's arrival, and in less than a month he named him the Prince Kan and entrusted him with the management of the political affairs for the whole kingdom. Afterwards Chen Yucheng was given the title the Prince Ying in recognition of his outstanding war service and several other princes were appointed. Thus the leadership nucleus for the latter period was formed.

Hung Jen-kan's long sojourns in Hongkong and elsewhere had brought him closely in contact with the science and culture of the capitalist West, and he had a good understanding of the world situation. Knowing of the rapid progress made by Western capitalist countries he hoped that China might undergo a transformation and catch up with the latest world developments. Later on, having drawn together and analysed all he had seen during his months in the capital, he formulated an overall political programme contained in his *New Guide to Government*.

The *New Guide to Government* opened with an explanation of the development and transformation of things. The principle of the whole programme was that things should be done in accordance with the time and the situation. Its basic ideas were concerned with "the employment of personnel" and "formulation of policies," for Hung Jen-kan thought that upon these two matters hung the prosperity of a nation. In relation to the employment of personnel, he advocated "strengthening the foundation," by which he meant building up strong central power, and wanted to ban cliques. factionalist alliances and self-interested groupings within the revolutionary ranks. He raised this to combat the divisive factionalism which still existed among the Taipings. Explaining the need for vigilance, he said, "All monsters and ghosts are mischief makers," and warned that being disruptive, they could do a great deal of harm to the revolution.

Concerning "formulation of policies," Hung Jenkan drawing on the experience of Western capitalist countries, put forward a whole set of proposals for political, economic and social reform, which are the essence of the *New Guide to Government*. In the political sphere he advocated the centralization of power, and the development of public opinion and communication between the authorities and the masses by means of newspapers and "confidential report boxes." He suggested that local government should be run autonomously through the "local officials" and "council of scholars" and that money and grain storehouses should be set up and should practise an accounting system. He recommended the cleaning up of the government service by prohibiting private dealings with officials and the sale of official posts or ranks, and the reform of the penal system by treating minor criminals leniently and making public the crimes of major criminals before they were punished. In the economic sphere he called for the development of transport and communications by such means as railway and highway construction, the use of steamers, the improvement of waterways; the establishment of a postal administration and a proper financial system by opening banks, issuing paper currency, popularizing insurance and so on. He urged that mines be opened, irrigation works built, technical innovations rewarded and so on. All this would have prepared the road for the development of a capitalist economy. In the social sphere he proposed various undertakings to encourage culture and good health: the promotion of schools, newspapers and hospitals; rewards for philanthropic enterprises and the establishment of social welfare and charity organizations such as homes for the blind, the lame, the deaf and the dumb, and for orphans, foundlings and widows. He wanted to prohibit feudal superstition, advising that all temples, monasteries and such superstitious practices as divination be abolished, that monks and nuns be secularized, and that the evil practices like the sale, or use of slaves or bondmaids, and female infanticide by drowning be forbidden. He also wanted to do away with bad customs like foot-binding, the use of gold and jade ornamentation, the raising of birds and crickets, and general dawdling away of time. The intention behind such reforms was to transform the backward decadence of the feudal way of life, and to set up an organized society, full of vigour.

After comparing and analysing conditions in various countries, Hung Jen-kan concluded that China should follow the example set by Britain and the United States in order to become more prosperous. He favoured trade and cultural relations with capitalist countries but opposed intervention by foreign powers in internal affairs, saying they should not be allowed to force their way inland in China without permission, or to violate the law of the Taiping Heavenly Kingdom. Opposing the arrogant national chauvinism of the Ching ruling class he said that phrases such as "coming from myriad countries to pay homage," "the submission of barbarians from the four corners of the earth" and derogatory terms like "barbarians" "savages" and "devils," should not be used. Moreover, he advocated intercourse with other countries on a basis of equality.

Hung Hsiu-chuan thought very highly of the *New Guide to Government*. Annotating it, he wrote "true," or "this is a good policy," against many points. He disagreed with only two of its proposals, the establishment of a news office and the abolition of the death penalty. Of the news office whose purpose was to collect news and reports from all over the country he said: "This policy cannot be implemented at present, for the monsters might seize the opportunity to sow discord. It must wait until all the monsters have been killed." Of the death penalty he commented: "We kill the evil to protect the righteous. Killing monsters and criminals is necessary." This demonstrates Hung Hsiu-chuan's vigilance against the enemy and his firm adhesion to the revolution. The *New Guide to Government* was printed and promulgated with Hung Hsiu-chuan's careful annotations, so it could be said that the ideals advanced in it to learn from the West or to develop what is now known as capitalism were also among Hung Hsiu-chuan's precepts.

Although the *New Guide to Government* was publicly promulgated, it was difficult to implement in the crisis-ridden atmosphere of war. Moreover, as a complete political programme, it had shortcomings and limitations: It did not touch on the land problem which had already been raised in the *Heavenly Land System*, and besides, it regarded invaders from capitalist countries who were in fact aggressors, as "upholding faith and righteousness." Nevertheless, the *New Guide to Government* was really significant as a political programme and had some ideological influence. While Hung Jen-kan held power, he did his best to overcome the dangerous disunity amongst the leadership. He criticized those officials crazy for rank who, regarding promotion as glory, felt that it was slow progress to get nine promotions a year and were even dissatisfied with three a month. He maintained that "a piece of writing should record something real," approving a "clear, realistic style which can be easily understood," and condemning "flowery descriptions" and "meaningless empty words," which he said restricted people's ideas and were better left unread. He made a great effort to break down feudal superstition, urging people not to worship that "stupid man-made dead monster — the Buddha." He described Buddhas as monsters, lifeless things of wood, clay, stone or paper and said, "They can neither see with their eyes, speak with their mouths, work with their hands, nor walk with their feet." All were false and intended to deceive people. Trying to alert people by using a popular verse style he wrote:

Idols of metal, stone, wood and clay
Which people worship every day
Have a form which might look real,
But it's quite false, they cannot feel.
Temples solemnly decked out you know
Appear so grand to make a show.

All this was a partial implementation of his new political programme. In his emphasis on destroying the old and fostering the new in culture he can be seen as a herald of the new culture movement in modern China.

9

The Siege of the Heavenly Capital Is Raised Again and the Eastward Advance

The dangerous military situation continued after Hung Jen-kan was entrusted with important military and political posts. The capital was under pressure from Hochun and Chang Kuo-liang's besieging forces at the Great South Camp. Their trenches extended for miles around, and they were encamped in over 100 strongholds and outposts. Furthermore, the lower Yangtze was blockaded by Ching gunboats. The situation was even graver than it had been when Hsiang Jung had laid siege to the capital. This time the city could not be relieved merely by launching offensives. At the beginning of 1860, Hung Jen-kan proposed an original strategy of surprise attack. He said: "Besieged as we are, it is difficult to make a strong offensive. We should make an attack on the enemy rear at Huchow and Hangchow in Chekiang, where their forces are rather weak, then, they will pull back to reinforce Huchow and Hangchow. Once they have gone, we can rush troops back to save ourselves here. In this way we should win a great victory." His idea was that if they could draw the Ching troops away by attack on their rear they could then make a successful attack on the Great South Camp.

Following this plan, Li Hsiu-cheng and Li Shih-hsien marched on Hangchow and Huchow. When they captured Hangchow in February, just as Hung Jen-kan had foreseen, over 13,000 men were sent from the Great South Camp to retake the town. As the enemy reinforcements neared Hangchow, the Taiping Army set up banners inside and outside the city to delude the enemy, and then promptly evacuated it and marched quickly back through south Anhwei. In April, Chen Yu-cheng, Li Hsiu-cheng, Li Shih-hsien, Yang Fu-ching, Liu Kuan-fang and other commanders joined forces in Anhwei at Chienping (present-day Langhsi) and made a plan to divide up again and march to the capital by five different routes.

The war to raise the siege of the Heavenly Capital began on May 2. Approaching from every direction the Taipings were able to surround the Ching troops from the outer perimeter, while their forces within the city sallied out to attack their besiegers. Hochun and Chang Kuo-liang, the commanders of the Great South Camp, could not take the pressure and kept retreating. Chen Yu-cheng's troops destroyed the trenches southwest of the capital, and this was followed up with a general offensive from all the Taiping positions. On May 6, they smashed over 50 Ching camps and posts between the Tesheng Gate of the Heavenly Capital and the Yangtze River. Hochun and Chang Kuo-liang fled with the remnants of their forces to Chenkiang. Thus, the Taiping Army smashed the Great South Camp for the second time, and raised the three-year siege of the city.

Five days after the relief of the Heavenly Capital, on May 11, Hung Jen-kan, Chen Yu-cheng, Li Hsiu-cheng, Li Shih-hsien and Yang Fu-ching had an audience with Hung Hsiu-chuan at the Palace of the Heavenly King to discuss what strategy should be employed to ensure them continued victories. Chen Yu-cheng thought that the main force should be sent westwards to deal with the Ching troops gathering in northwest Anhwei, which he considered a threat to Anking. Li Shih-hsien on the other hand wanted an eastward advance so that they might expand towards Chekiang and Fukien through the prosperous region of the lower Yangtze valley. Combining these two views, Hung Jen-kan pointed out that the Soochow, Hangchow and Shanghai areas were not far from the capital and that after the recent Taiping victories, an expedition straight down the Yangtze was likely to succeed. Once in control of the lower Yangtze, the Taipings could make use of its manpower and products in a campaign to take Kiangsi and Hupeh on the middle Yangtze. Thus they would hold both banks of the river, and the enemy would not be able to keep up its pressure on Anking. Hung Hsiu-chuan agreed with Hung Jen-kan's suggestion, so it was decided that they should advance first eastwards, then westwards. This was a correct general strategy; its ultimate failure was due to the intervention of the foreign aggressors, which had not been foreseen at the start.

On May 15, Li Hsiu-cheng, Li Shih-hsien and Yang Fu-ching led a great army eastwards. The troops gathered by Hochun and Chang Kuo-liang to defend Tanyang, which the Taipings reached on May 17, were routed completely. Chang Kuo-liang was wounded and fled, but his mount slipped into the river, so man and horse were both drowned. Hochun fled to Hsushukuan near Soochow, where in his fear, he committed suicide, swallowing opium with strong liquor. The Taiping Army then went on to take Changchow and Wusih. On June 2, with the support of the Small Sword Society from inside the city, they took the provincial capital, Soochow, without a fight. Next, they captured the towns of Kiangyin, Wukiang, Kunshan, Taitsang, Chiating, Chingpu, Sungkiang in southern Kiangsu, and Chiahsing in Chekiang. Another column under Chen Yu-cheng from Yihsing in southern Kiangsu took Yuchien, Linan and Yuhang in Chekiang as they pressed on to Hangchow. In less than two months, after hard fighting the Taipings conquered a large area on the lower Yangtze. They established a province called "Sufu" containing more than 20 sub-prefectures and counties with Soochow as its capital.

Just as the Taipings' eastern expedition was moving victoriously on towards Shanghai after having taken Soochow and many other towns, the foreign aggressors brazenly intervened to check their advance. To reach a clear understanding of this turn of affairs it is necessary to recall the whole history of foreign intervention against the revolutionary Taiping Heavenly Kingdom.

As soon as the Taiping Army began its victorious march on the Yangtze valley, the British-owned *North China Herald*, published weekly at Shanghai, advocated open support for the Ching government and intervention against the Taiping Revolution in order to suppress it. It claimed in its editorial on January 15, 1853, that the revolution's "ultimate success will be the signal for hostile measures against foreigners in China; we have thus much to lose and nothing to gain by the subversion of the Ta-Tsing [Ching] dynasty. . . ."*

This newspaper reflected the intentions of the British government. On January 13 that year, Sir John Rutherford Alcock, the British consul in Shanghai, had proposed in his secret correspondence with Sir George Bonham, Governor of Hongkong and concurrently plenipotentiary to China, that the British occupy Chenkiang immediately and send their fleet to blockade the Grand Canal and the Yangtze's tributaries. Alcock explained that "coercive measures" must be "adopted to ensure success in any negotiations with the Chinese Government."** Alcock had for long been secretly harbouring such thoughts and his idea was that to make things look right, the Ching government should invite armed intervention. In February that year, having received a note from the Governor of Kiangsu asking for aid, he wrote Bonham a report in which he proposed the immediate suppression of the Taiping Revolution, either by British armed forces acting alone, or by joint British, French and American action, in order to secure from the Ching

* *North China Herald,* January 15, 1853.

** Alexander Michie: *The Englishman in China,* London, 1900, Vol. I, p. 428.

government remunerations for the intervention, unrestricted access to all inland and coastal ports, direct diplomatic relations with Peking and the legalization of opium. In March, Bonham came to Shanghai with a fleet to negotiate some sort of return to be made for an attack on the Taiping Heavenly Kingdom with the Viceroy of the Liang-kiang Provinces.

But, the invaders' ideas were overtaken by events. Two days before Bonham's arrival at Shanghai, the Taipings captured Nanking, the most important city in southeast China, and immediately afterwards took Chenkiang. The plan of attack which the invaders had made was completely upset.

After the proclamation of the Heavenly Capital, envoys from various capitalist countries visited it to gather news and intelligence. The British envoy Bonham went at the end of April 1853, the French envoy Alphonse de Bourboulon, in December, and the American envoy Robert McLane, in May the following year.

When Bonham arrived at the Heavenly Capital, he gave the Taipings a translation of the Treaty of Nanking, intending to force them to accept the unequal treaty. He threatened that if the Taiping Army or anyone else should in any way inflict harm on the lives and property of the British residents, Britain would resort to the measures it employed

10 years ago. De Bourboulon not only insisted on the treaty provisions, he also brought up the question of the protection of the Roman Catholic Church. McLane said that "citizens of the United States, residing in China, under the guarantees of a solemn Treaty, were much exposed, both in their persons and property, by the civil strife,"* and he demanded that the Taipings respect their privileges.

After these three envoys had visited the Heavenly Capital and seen the superior military might of the Taipings, judging that they might possibly gain power nationally, they adopted for a time a wait-and-see policy, remaining "neutral" until they saw how things would go. Should the northern expedition prove successful, they could establish relations with the Taipings; should it fail, they might be in a position to bargain with the Ching government and extort more privileges. In his report to the British Foreign Office Bonham wrote: ". . . should we assist the present government and the Rebels ultimately succeed, our position in China would be most embarrassing." Therefore, "it is the wisest, if not the only, policy to wait some time longer. . . ." Bonham's proposal was formally approved by the Foreign Office, and the French and

---

* *North China Herald*, No. 202, June 10, 1854.

American governments adopted the same policy of "neutrality."

In September 1853, inspired by the Taiping Revolution the Small Sword Society led a rising and occupied Shanghai, then a county town. With the collaboration of the Governor of Kiangsu, the foreign aggressors built a wall to separate the "concessions" from the county town of Shanghai, thus cutting the Small Sword Society's supply line. Meanwhile their warships bombarded the walled city, slaughtering both insurgents and civilians and they seized the chance to take over the powers of the Chinese Customs. The Customs House in Shanghai was burnt down after the Small Sword uprising. The Circuit Intendant of Shanghai Wu Chien-chang, escaped into the "concessions," and the Customs ceased to function. The British invaders did all they could to obstruct the rebuilding of the Customs House, and foreign merchant-ships stopped paying duties, so that Shanghai became a "free port" for them. In June 1854, the foreign consuls signed a customs agreement with Wu Chien-chang. Britain, France and the United States were each to appoint an officer to supervise the collection of dues. Thus the Shanghai Customs House slipped into their hands, opening the era of foreign capitalist control of the Chinese Customs. This not only extended the range of powers they had seized in Shanghai, by striking at the Taiping Heavenly Kingdom, it obstructed the cause of popular revolution in China.

In October 1856, the British and French with Russian and American support, launched the Second Opium War, and in 1858 they compelled the Ching government to sign the Treaties of Tientsin, which forced the opening of all the ports along the Yangtze, and exacted concessions which the Taipings would never have made. By this time the Taipings' northern expedition had failed, and their power was confined to the middle and lower Yangtze regions which greatly interested the foreign invaders and which they were keen to open. In November 1858, Lord Elgin, the British ambassador-extraordinary, commanded British warships to sail westwards upstream from Shanghai. In defiance of the Taiping prohibition they swept up past the Heavenly Capital, Wuhu and Anking, shelling as they went until they reached Hankow. On their way back, they anchored near the Heavenly Capital while some of them landed to negotiate and reconnoitre. The foreign aggressors then felt that the wait-and-see period was over, that all was clear and that the time had come to pull off the veil of neutrality and intervene openly against the Taiping Revolution.

On May 26, 1860, at the height of the Taipings' successes in the lower Yangtze region, just as they were preparing to attack Shanghai, the British envoy Sir Frederick Bruce, and the French envoy de Bourboulon, made a joint declaration that they would defend Shanghai by force of arms. To impede the Taipings' attack on Shanghai, they openly put the town under their "protection." Bruce sent many reports to the British Foreign Office, denigrating the Taiping Army as a host of bandits, claiming that most of its followers came from the dangerous class in China, and that they were ceaselessly demolishing faith, wealth and trade and so on, trying to justify their intervention. Bruce, an agent of Western aggression hostile to the Taipings, now openly made military preparations for armed intervention. In an express letter to the British Foreign Secretary, Lord John Russell, Bruce wrote that he had decided to use both the navy and the army to stop the "bloodshed" and "plunder." In fact, he was resolved to strangle the revolution in China.

Another step taken by the foreign interventionalists was the formation of Ward's "Foreign Rifle Detachment" in June 1860. Frederick Townsend Ward was born in the United States at Salem, Massachusetts. He attended military school when young and then drifted abroad, living as a soldier adventurer in Mexico and France. Having heard about the Taiping Revolution and the prolonged war in China, he thought it a fine chance to seek his fortune. So in 1859, he made his way alone to Shanghai. He soon made contact with a compradore called Yang Fang, a candidate circuit intendant and one of the directors of the Association of Ningpoese in Shanghai. Yang Fang introduced Ward to Wu Hsu, intendant of the Soochow-Sungkiang-Taitsang circuit. Ward expressed his willingness to recruit a foreign army to fight the Taipings. As these compradores and bureaucrats were seeking the aid of foreigners, they quickly reached agreement. Ward was to recruit and train the men, Wu Hsu and Yang Fang would supply arms, finance the army, and reward the capture of each city richly. So Ward, having recruited 200 foreigners and a few hundred Chinese, set up his infamous "Foreign Rifle Detachment," which he commanded, assisted by two more American mercenaries, Henry Burgevine and Edward Forrester. These foreigners were riffraff who had come to China to seek fortune and adventure and who had lived in the Shanghai "concessions" for many years.

In July, scarcely one month after its formation, the "Foreign Rifle Detachment" set out in boats to make a night assault on Sungkiang. The Taipings hit back hard, Ward was wounded and the whole detachment fell back in confusion to Shanghai, where Ward reorganized his forces, equipping them with a large quantity of new weapons. Backed up by 7,000 Ching soldiers in their rear, they initiated another assault on Sungkiang in mid-July. The Taipings fought bravely, stubbornly defending the inner city wall after the outer one had been breached. The rifles of the "Foreign Rifle Detachment" were powerless against this wall, but finally Ward and his men crept in through a hole and took the city for which Ward got a reward of 133,000 silver dollars.

Ward was applauded by reactionaries, foreign and Chinese alike, for his capture of Sungkiang, and lost all sense of reality in his arrogance. In early August he led the "Foreign Rifle Detachment" with 10,000 Ching back-up troops, in two assaults on Chingpu. Both attacks failed, the second disastrously. The detachment suffered 200-300 men killed or wounded, and the Ching troops' casualties were much higher. Moreover, the Taipings captured a quantity of foreign-made guns and rifles. Ward himself was wounded, this time seriously, and had to be carried back to Sungkiang in a covered sedan followed by the tattered remnants of his forces. The Taiping Army pursued them right up to the city walls, giving the foreign invaders a taste of their strength.

However, the foreigners' intervention and the damage they did, did not put Li Hsiu-cheng, the leader of the eastern expeditionary army, on his guard. Late in June, not long after the Taipings captured Soochow, Li Hsiu-cheng wrote to the British Minister in Shanghai, explaining the necessity for the Taipings to take Sungkiang and march on Shanghai, and inviting the British and other ministers to come to Soochow to negotiate "a new present-day alliance." Not only did this letter fail to elicit a proper response, it gave the foreign invaders a precise notification of the Taipings' proposed attack on Shanghai, hastening their defence preparations. On July 10, Li Hsiu-cheng wrote another letter to the British, French and American ministers, in which, although he mentioned that in the river at Sungkiang "three or five foreign ships are bombarding ceaselessly," and that within the city of Shanghai foreign soldiers "were assisting the devil's defence," he still expressed the hope that the foreign invaders would "behave with sincerity" by which he meant they should withdraw voluntarily.

Having defeated Ward's "Foreign Rifle Detachment" at Chingpu, the Taipings attacked Shanghai on August 17 as they had planned, and cleared the city outskirts of Ching troops. The next day, Li Hsiu-cheng, still harbouring all sorts of delusions, notified the ministers of various foreign countries that when the Taiping Army entered Shanghai, no foreigners would be harmed providing that they put yellow banners up on their roofs to distinguish themselves. On that same day, he led a small force of 3,000 men to Hsuchiahui in the belief that they might get into Shanghai without much of a fight. But, when the Taipings reached the city gate there were no yellow banners flying, instead they saw foreign soldiers standing on the city walls, their rifles trained on the Heavenly Army. Then bullets rained down on them. Still seeking an understanding with his "foreign brothers," Li Hsiu-cheng ordered his troops to retreat without firing back. The expeditionary army suffered heavy casualties and its assault upon its final goal was frustrated by foreign intervention.

Nevertheless, the year of 1860 marked the peak of success for the Taiping Heavenly Kingdom in its latter period.

Before and After the Defensive Battle of Anking

10

After the Taipings' eastern expedition had ended, they began a second expedition to the west. Its ultimate objective was Wuhan, for strategically they hoped that if their army could win some victories in the upper Yangtze area it would break up the encirclement of Anking.

Since the fall of Kiukiang in May 1858, the Hunan troops had been gradually tightening their grip in both north and south Anhwei. The defence of the Heavenly Capital in the upper area turned on Anking. If something happened to it, the Ching troops would be able to drive straight down to the Taiping capital itself. Hung Jen-kan, making use of an ancient metaphor, compared the Yangtze River to a long snake with Hupeh as its head, Anhwei, its waist and Kiangsu and Chekiang, its tail. He said: "At present, Hupeh has not yet been conquered; if Anhwei should fall, the snake would be severed in the middle and its tail, though alive, could not last very long." This most graphically described the strategic position of Anhwei.

Tseng Kuo-fan thought that the key to defeating the Taipings would be the capture of Anking. During the first half of 1860, when the Taipings had smashed the Great South Camp and were mopping up the Soochow and Changchow areas, the panic-stricken Ching government dismissed Ho Kuei-ching, the Viceroy of the Liangkiang Provinces, and put him to death. Tseng Kuo-fan was appointed in his place, at first as acting Viceroy, but the appointment was formalized in less than two months and he was made concurrently Imperial Commissioner for military affairs in the lower Yangtze while all ground and river forces both north and south of the Yangtze were put under his command. In other words he was given full military authority to suppress the Taiping Revolution. The Ching government urged him to rush the Hunan Army to the Kiangsu and Chekiang battlefields in order to recover Soochow and Changchow and to safeguard Shanghai and Hangchow. But Tseng Kuo-fan, whose eyes were fixed on Anking, explained his counter-revolutionary plan to the Emperor, saying: "Since ancient times, the strategy for pacifying the lower Yangtze has been to establish a strong position in the upper region, and then to press downstream. Only in this way can success be ensured." In other words, he regarded Anking as a vantage point from which to seize Nanking and therefore firmly refused to transfer his troops from this front. The Hunan troops were putting pressure on Anking from three directions. Hu Lin-yi had established a big camp for his army in Taihu County from which to direct military affairs in northern Anhwei. Tseng Kuo-fan chose Chimen in south Anhwei as his headquarters so that he appeared to be going to march on Soochow and Changchow, but his real intention was to obstruct Taiping troops coming to the relief of Anking from the south. Tseng Kuo-fan's cunning arrangements were based on the idea that the only way to secure the dangerous situation was to capture Anking.

In accordance with their original plan, and also in view of troop dispositions on both sides, the Taipings decided in September 1860 to advance west in two separate columns. One army under Chen Yu-cheng was to march up the northern bank of the Yangtze from Anhwei to Hupeh, while the other under Li Hsiu-cheng advanced south of the Yangtze through Kiangsi to Hupeh, co-ordinating their attacks with forces under Li Shih-hsien, Yang Fu-ching and others. The two armies were to join forces at Wuhan, the triple city composed of Hankow, Hanyang and Wuchang, in April 1861.

The north route army under Chen Yu-cheng fought its way bravely along the northern bank of the Yangtze through northern Anhwei and from Huoshan into Hupeh. In March 1861, they captured Huangchow (present-day Huangkang), only about 50 kilometres from Hankow, intending to turn the city into a strategic base for the operations against Wuhan. But as soon as the Taipings arrived at Huangchow, the foreign invaders began to murmur with discontent.

Meanwhile, Sir Harry Parkes, a British consul who had come up to Hankow to gather intelligence on the situation along the Yangtze, went to Huangchow, accompanied by two British merchants, to meet Chen Yu-cheng. Chen was told that the three cities of Wuchang, Hankow and Hanyang formed a gigantic emporium, the trade of which would be damaged if the Taipings seized any one of the cities. He was therefore advised to keep away from them. Taking advantage of the fact that the north and the south route armies were not in contact with each other, Parkes falsely claimed that the south route army had not yet entered Kiangsi, and tried to intimidate Chen Yu-cheng by pointing out that without the support of the other armies Chen would have to cope unaided with the Ching defence forces at Wuchang and simultaneously with the Anhwei troops assailing his rear. Parkes' intervention made Chen Yu-cheng hesitate. He postponed the offensive against Wuhan and sent a messenger back to the capital to ask for instructions. When the time came for the two armies to meet, Chen Yu-cheng had still heard nothing from Li Hsiu-cheng. Anxious to go to the rescue of Anking, he withdrew his forces to Anhwei in mid-April, leaving Lai Wen-kuang to defend Huangchow. When the order to advance on Wuhan according to the original plan arrived from the capital, Chen Yu-cheng had already left Hupeh.

Why had the south route army under Li Hsiu-cheng not arrived in Hupeh on time? The decision to send the two-pronged expedition to the west had been made in September, but Li Hsiu-cheng lingered around his strongholds in the Soochow-Changchow area, delaying his departure until October. He fought a few engagements with the Hunan Army in southern Anhwei and by the end of the year he was very near to Tseng Kuo-fan's headquarters at Chimen. Tseng Kuo-fan bewailed that the Taipings were only 40 kilometres away and that starting in the morning they could arrive by evening, for there was nothing to hold them back. He sighed deeply that he passed every day in tempest and storm. At the height of the danger, he told his subordinates that anyone who wanted to go might do so. Prepared to meet his end he wrote a 2,000-word testament and sent it to his family. Quite unexpectedly, Li Hsiu-cheng, loath to fight a hard battle, skirted around Tseng's camp, leaving him untouched. On their march from Kiangsi to Hupeh, Li Hsiu-cheng ignored the appointed date for the rendezvous, losing a lot of time recruiting large numbers of new soldiers from various places to expand his own power. His army arrived in the counties of Hsingkuo and Wuchang (present-day Ocheng) in June 1861, two months after they were due, when Chen Yu-cheng, unable to make contact with them, had already returned to northern Anhwei with his army.

Nevertheless, the south route army captured Tungshan, Tungcheng, Chiayu, Puchi, Hsienning and many strongholds on the outskirts of Wuchang. Learning of this, Hu Lin-yi had to lead his men back westwards from Taihu County in Anhwei to save Wuchang. This affected the general disposition of the Hunan troops in north Anhwei and left the situation more fluid than before. But Li Hsiu-cheng was induced by Gingell, the British consul at Hankow whom he met in Hsingkuo, to give up the idea of attacking Wuhan. He asked Gingell to carry two important letters he had written to Chen Yu-cheng and Lai Wen-kuang on his voyage downstream from Hankow. In fact Gingell kept these two letters, and later they were acquired by the British Museum. The troops under Li Hsiu-cheng's command now numbered 500,000. If in co-ordination with Lai Wen-kuang who was still at Huangchow he had launched a strong attack on Wuchang, it might have influenced the whole disposition of the enemy forces. Even if it had been impossible to take Wuchang immediately, the pressure on Anking could have been relieved and the Taipings might have regained the initiative. But, Li Hsiu-cheng, wishing to preserve his military strength for his own stalking grounds in Kiangsu and Chekiang, abandoned his mission to take Wuhan in spite of the general strategic significance of the task and pulled his troops back precipitately to Kiangsi and Chekiang dissipating all chances of victory on the upper Yangtze. Even the enemy was surprised that Li Hsiu-cheng withdrew without a fight. A few years later, in his interrogation he was asked why when he reached Hupeh, instead of withdrawing he had not tried to raise the siege of Anking by attacking Wuchang. Li Hsiu-cheng stammered out that it had been a miscalculation, "due perhaps to the will of Heaven."

After the failure of the plan to launch a joint attack on Wuhan the Taipings had no choice but to accept a life-and-death struggle at Anking. In April 1861, arriving back in northern Anhwei from

Hupeh, Chen Yu-cheng led his army straight to the defence of Anking.

Anking had been under siege for a year. Tseng Kuo-chuan had had deep trenches dug, and high ramparts and forts constructed everywhere. Three great trenches enclosed Anking, one to impede sorties by the Taipings within the city, one to cut them off from reinforcements and one to protect the attackers' rear. Tolunga and Li Hsu-yi each with a force of over 10,000 men were stationed separately around Tungcheng to watch out for the approach of Taiping reinforcements from that city; Pao Chao's force of over 5,000 men was quartered on the river bank opposite Anking and Yang Tsai-fu's river forces held numerous strategic points along the Yangtze ready to give support. This massive encirclement of Anking was intended to crush it.

Chen Yu-cheng arrived from Hupeh to give aid late in April. When he neared Chihsienkuan he launched an attack on the Hunan troops besieging Anking. Hung Jen-kan and Lin Shao-chang led armies from the Heavenly Capital to Lientan near Anking joining forces en route with Wu Ju-hsiao's troops. The battle for the control of Anking began. The front lines of the two armies were locked together in jagged rings of encirclement and counter-encirclement. Hung Jen-kan's relief forces were unable to get the upper hand of the besiegers in the course of several fierce engagements in May, and then, in early June, the camps at Chihsienkuan and Chihkangling, formerly held by the brave general Liu Chiang-lin, fell into enemy hands. The Taiping Army suffered heavy losses and was left at a disadvantage.

To meet this crisis, Chen Yu-cheng reorganized the relief forces and launched an attack on Anking in August together with Yang Fu-ching, Lin Shao-chang, Wu Ju-hsiao, Huang Wen-chin and other generals. After many days of hard struggle, they took Chihsienkuan and broke through the first line of the enemy trenches. The Taiping garrison commanders ordered over 10 sorties out of the city to try to link up with Chen Yu-cheng's army but all to no avail. Then the city ran out of grain. On September 5, 1861, the Ching troops mined Anking's west gate and destroyed it. The whole garrison of over 16,000 and its commanders, Yeh Yun-lai and Wu Ting-tsai fought on to the last, finally laying down their lives for the revolutionary cause. Thus ended the fierce and tragic battle to defend Anking. The revolutionary spirit of the Taiping defenders who stood firm, and fearless in the face of death was truly admirable.

After the fall of Anking, the defeated Taiping Army was pursued and harried everywhere. At the same time Tseng Kuo-chuan led an advance on the Heavenly Capital. The situation was critical. Nevertheless, Chen Yu-cheng and his commanders Lai Wen-kuang and Chen Teh-tsai carried on the fight in north Anhwei, while Yang Fu-ching, Huang Wen-chin and Liu Kuan-fang held out firmly in the south of the province. Had Li Hsiu-cheng left his Chekiang command to Li Shih-hsien and led his men to the Anhwei battlefront, the Taipings would have been able to rally their forces on the upper Yangtze. But Li Hsiu-cheng stuck wilfully to his own projects in Kiangsu and Chekiang, ignoring the vital matter of safeguarding the Heavenly Capital. On withdrawing from Hupeh, he had gone straight to Chekiang, showing no concern at all for the critical situation in the battle to defend Anking, nor, after its fall, had he attempted to make amends. Hung Jen-kan wrote to him reproachfully that although the upper Yangtze was vital to the capital's defence, he was only interested in the prosperous cities of Soochow and Hangchow and ignored the situation in Anhwei. He prophesied that should something happen, they would not be able to hold out very long, and expressed the hope that Li would change his plans and come to the relief of Anhwei. Li Hsiu-cheng said in his reply: "At present, the situation is not favourable for defeating the enemy.

Similarly, when you eat fruit before the proper time, it tastes sour." On this pretext he refused to obey orders.

The fall of Anking made Hung Hsiu-chuan very anxious. He dismissed Hung Jen-kan and Chen Yu-cheng for their failure to save Anking. Thereafter the management of state affairs fell more to Hung Jen-fa and Hung Jen-ta, and many more titles were awarded. In the following two or three years, 200 or more princes were appointed, a practice which had bad repercussions on the relationships between the ranks in the Taiping Army.

Hung Jen-kan and Chen Yu-cheng were not disheartened by the loss of Anking, they spurred themselves on with their setbacks, and kept on fighting courageously. Hung Jen-kan wrote two essays entitled "On the Extermination of Monsters" on the situation produced by the defeat. In them he denounced the crimes of the Ching rulers, calling on people to "leave darkness for enlightenment" so that all could contribute to the revolution. He also advocated that in the revolutionary ranks "old and new brothers should all be regarded as a united whole." All this was proclaimed both inside and outside the army to revive people's will to fight and raise their revolutionary morale. After retreating to Luchow, Chen Yu-cheng made efforts to reorganize and revitalize his forces in preparation for an advance to the north to try to alter the situation. Even before the Battle of Anking, Chen Yu-cheng had wished to campaign in the north. A group of men familiar with conditions there had already been sent to work in Shantung and Chihli, setting up secret communications networks and trying to recruit agents in the enemy ranks. After a period of recuperation and reorganization, Lai Wen-kuang, Chen Teh-tsai and Ma Jung-ho joined Chang Lo-hsing, the leader of the Nien fighters, and marched to Honan in January 1862. Chen Yu-cheng himself then decided to follow them with an army.

While Chen Yu-cheng was making new military arrangements, the Hunan troops under Tolunga and Li Hsu-yi began a siege of Luchow in February. After an encirclement and counter-encirclement campaign lasting three months, Chen Yu-cheng, seeing that he was cut off from outside reinforcements, broke through the enemy lines with 4,000 seasoned troops and sped north. He intended to make contact with Miao Pei-lin at Shouchow (present-day Shouhsien) in Anhwei, regroup his forces, and then push forward. Miao Pei-lin, formerly the captain of a landlord militia corps, had come over to the Taipings and put himself under Chen Yu-cheng's command as a result of dissension within the corps. Meanwhile, however, this rogue had maintained secret connections with the Ching general Shengpao. He pretended he would welcome Chen Yu-cheng to Shouchow, so Chen unsuspectingly marched into the city with only a handful of followers. Miao Pei-lin treacherously captured him and sent him to the Ching camp. There, Shengpao ordered him to kneel. He indignantly refused, reminding him: "You fled every battle. At Paishihshan, where 50 of your encampments were destroyed, and your whole army annihilated, you fled in terror with a dozen mounts. I ordered that your life be spared. Why should I kneel to a rascal so lacking in self-respect?" He added, "But for Miao Pei-lin's trick, I would never have been captured." When Shengpao continued to urge submission, Chen Yu-cheng cried out fearlessly, "Cease this nonsense. I want to die like a man." Shengpao wanted to parade his success so he sent Chen to Peking under guard, but his escort, hearing that the Taiping and Nien armies planned to ambush them en route, killed their prisoner at Yenchin in Honan on June 4, 1862. At the time of his death he was only 26.

Chen Yu-cheng was an outstanding young Taiping general who proved steadfastly loyal to the last. He gave up his young life for the revolutionary Taiping cause. His death was an irredeemable loss to the Taipings.

Meanwhile, the situation in the southeast had not been static. In May 1861, at the most critical point in the battle to defend Anking, Li Shih-hsien had marched into Chekiang from Kiangsi. In two or three months, he took many towns, among them Changshan, Suian, Chuchow, Lungyu and Chinhua, and occupied most of western and southern Chekiang. Retreating from Hupeh, Li Hsiu-cheng had also entered Chekiang by way of Kiangsi right after the fall of Anking. He besieged Hangchow and sent a detachment to attack Shaohsing from Hsiaoshan, and drive on to Ningpo. Ningpo, the important trading port in east Chekiang, was taken on December 9 that year, and Hangchow, the provincial capital, was captured on December 29. By then, most of Chekiang was in the hands of the Taipings.

These lightning Taiping successes in Chekiang were a great blow to the enemy. Tseng Kuo-fan bemoaned, "The whole province is rotten, nothing can be done there." Yet these victories could not compensate for the fall of Anking in the upper Yangtze region. Later on Li Shih-hsien said regretfully, "Our first error was to advance into Chekiang last year instead of defending Anhwei." Li Hsiu-cheng, as the commanding general of the south route army, bears the responsibility for the failure to carry out the overall military strategy.

Furthermore, their gains were not stable ones. Li Hsiu-cheng had enlisted so many men in Hupeh and Kiangsi that the ranks of his army swelled to over 700,000, but quite a lot of landlord militia, bandits and rogues, sneaked in at this time. Even Tseng Kuo-fan, an enemy of the Taipings, said that Li Hsiu-cheng had recruited large numbers of deserters from the Ching and occupied exclusively the richest regions. This band of followers he enlisted looted and slaughtered on their victorious march to Chekiang, ruining the name of the Taiping Army among the population. Afterwards, these men very quickly turned traitor under the onslaught of the Ching troops, undermining the Taiping Army from inside.

When the Taiping Army was swarming over Chekiang, the river and ground forces of the Hunan troops pressed eastwards down the Yangtze towards the Heavenly Capital. Tseng Kuo-fan petitioned the Emperor to appoint Tso Tsung-tang to lead a force into Chekiang. Tso Tsung-tang from Hsiangyin in Hunan was a reactionary intellectual of the landlord class. He had caught Tseng Kuo-fan's attention and had been offered a post in the Hunan Army as Tseng's military adjutant. He was ordered to enlist some men, lead them to fight and gain counter-revolutionary war experience. As soon as Tso Tsung-tang reached Chekiang, he was appointed Governor of Chekiang and became the chief criminal in the suppression of the Taiping Army in that province.

Facing the Foreign Invaders in Battle Array

11

As early as in July and August 1860, the foreign invaders began their armed intervention against the Taiping Revolution in the Shanghai area. But, as the British and French allied forces were then waging a war of aggression in north China, and the Treaties of Tientsin had not been put into effect, they and the Ching government still distrusted each other. This was the case until, with the signing of the Conventions of Peking which ended the Second Opium War in October, the Ching government became completely subservient, and the opening of all the ports along the Yangtze and other special privileges gave the foreign invaders a vested interest, so they began a much more active intervention against the Taiping Revolution. Lord Palmerston, the British Prime Minister, soon spoke on his new policy towards China:

"The state of things [in China] is now altered, and those very hostilities which were found fault with have resulted in this — that we are now on the most friendly terms with the Government of China, and that we have access to the supreme Government from which we were before debarred by local and provincial authorities.... Look to the great extension of that commerce which is likely to arise if, by our friendly assistance, we should be able to place the internal arrangements of China on a more regular footing [meaning to help suppress the Taiping Heavenly Kingdom and restore the Ching rule in south China]."*

In other words he thought the British had extorted sufficient privileges from the Ching government to be able to extract China's wealth indefinitely if the Taiping Heavenly Kingdom were now suppressed. The wife of the French minister de Bourboulon, noted with excitement in her diary that the Taiping Heavenly Kingdom "will be completely suppressed and Prince Kung will take charge of the country, which will make future negotiations much easier."**

Yihsin, usually known as Prince Kung who presided over the signing of the Conventions of Peking with the foreign invaders, acted as regent after the death of his brother the Hsien Feng Emperor in 1861. He considered that the foreign invaders

---

* A. E. Hake: *Events in the Taeping Rebellion,* London, 1891, p. 86.

** M. et Mme de Bourboulon: *Voyage en Chine et en Mongolie,* pp. 61-62.

were but "injuries in the limbs" while the Taiping Heavenly Kingdom was "a disease of the vitals"; the foreign invaders should therefore be "quietly won over," in other words, the Ching should join hands with them to deal with the "disease of the vitals." This was why the foreign invaders favoured him. Tseng Kuo-fan memorialized the throne to the same effect, saying: "Since the foreigners want to help us suppress the rebellion, we do not need to refuse them." With this treacherous scheme to borrow foreign forces to kill Chinese, the Ching government began its collaboration with the invaders' armed intervention.

At the time of the Taiping Revolution the Chinese people's understanding of the Western capitalist powers was still only at the perceptual stage. The Taiping leaders, with the idea that foreigners observed the same religious forms as they did, treated them all, including the invaders, as "foreign brothers." Cherishing the illusion that "under Heaven there is one family, and within the four seas all are brothers; since there is no difference between peoples, there should be no discrimination,"* they believed that their just revolutionary cause could win foreign support. Nevertheless, the Taiping leaders never made any

---

* Letter to Bonham.

concessions concerning fundamental national interests. In 1860, when the Taipings' advance on Shanghai was checked by the foreign invaders they had showed their justified indignation in repeated protests. In the face of threats from the foreign aggressors, they stuck unflinchingly to their independent revolutionary road and began to struggle against them, rendering blow for blow.

Soon after the Conventions of Peking had been signed, Elgin, the British ambassador-extraordinary, who had once sneaked his warships into Hankow, instructed Admiral James Hope, the British naval commander-in-chief in Shanghai, that "a naval force, sufficiently large to inspire respect, should present itself before Nankin,"* — a move to intimidate the Taiping Heavenly Kingdom. In February 1861, six warships sailed up the Yangtze from the mouth of the Whangpoo River at Woosung. After they had reached the Heavenly Capital, Commander Aplin was sent to present a note to the Taipings to the effect that they had obtained the right to open up the Yangtze and that they were anchored at Nanking in pursuance of that right. Admiral Hope continued his reconnaissance mission to Hankow and on his return voyage, he wrote threateningly to the Taipings

---

* Quoted by Lin-le, p. 332.

again: "The Governments of England and France having ordered that any attempt of the Taeping army to enter Shanghae or Woo-sung shall be repelled by force; and it being clear, therefore, that the presence of the Taeping troops in that vicinity can be productive of no good to them, and may lead to collision, it is very desirable that they should not approach within two days' march of these places."* The foreign warships might lawlessly invade China's seas and rivers but the Chinese people were not allowed to rise up in revolt in their own country. This was the bandit logic of Western colonialism. The Taiping Army answered the unreasonable demands of the foreign invaders by launching a second attack at Shanghai.

Having captured Hangchow late in 1861, Tan Shao-kuang, the Prince Mu, and other Taiping generals grouped their troops for a new five-pronged advance on Shanghai from Soochow and Hangchow in January 1862. They publicly announced to people, both Chinese and foreign, in all walks of life that Shanghai must be recovered. They swiftly mopped up the Ching troops in the outer Shanghai region, defeated Ward's "Foreign Rifle Detachment" at Fenghsien and began a siege of Shanghai.

---

* Ibid., p. 334.

Early in 1862, upon the news that the Taipings were nearer to Shanghai, the panic-stricken reactionaries, both Chinese and foreign, immediately organized a "Sino-Foreign Defence Alliance" and began to lay their plans. As the Taipings intensified their offensive, the British and French troops divided Shanghai up into defence zones. In February, John Michel, a British general, led the 99th Regiment and a battery of artillery from Tientsin to Shanghai. Ward also hurried to Shanghai to contact the British and French commanders, hoping to expand his "Foreign Rifle Detachment." The foreign invaders thus openly organized counter-revolutionary allied forces to suppress the Taiping Revolution.

The Taiping heroes fought resolutely back against the foreign invaders who dared to intrude.

In February the Taiping Army entered the Putung area, hard by the city of Shanghai. They fought a furious battle with the allied forces of the invaders at Kaochiao in which Henry Burgevine was wounded and the Taipings also suffered losses. In another fierce engagement early in March 30 kilometres outside Shanghai at Hsiaotang, a shortage of fire-arms resulted in heavy casualties for the Taiping Army. Ward gained great advantage from these two battles, and henceforth reactionaries renamed his "Foreign Rifle Detachment" which so brutally slaughtered the revolutionary Chinese people the "Ever-Victorious Army."

Early in April, the allied forces of the invaders attacked Lochiakang, Chipao, Wangchiasha and other fronts. The Taipings met with setbacks in all these battles except at the stronghold of Lochiakang, 15 kilometres from Shanghai, where they held out bravely throwing back three ferocious assaults of the "Ever-Victorious Army" led by the dare-devil Ward. Deadly gun-fire poured down on the allied forces and the proud Admiral Hope was forced to give the order to retreat. As he did so a bullet hit him in the calf and he had to be carried back while his troops made a disordered retreat. On April 17 Ward, the British general C. W. Staveley and the French admiral A. L. Protet, led their forces in a fierce artillery attack on Choupu, 20 kilometres from Shanghai. Having occupied the Taiping barracks, these felons started to plunder everywhere and were soon arguing over their loot. To avoid a repetition of this disgraceful performance, the French and British commanders even drew up a "civilized" convention on plunder, laying down that no one should loot the occupied areas by themselves and that all booty should be equally divided.

From late April to mid-May, the allied forces of the aggressors frequently attacked Chiating, Chingpu, Fenghsien and other places. On May 17, an army numbering 4,600 deployed 30 heavy cannon against Nanchiaochen in Fenghsien. The Taiping garrison of 1,000 prepared to defend it firmly, building walls and digging trenches. Seeing that the town could not be taken by a charge, the enemy shelled the walls continually for two hours till they were shattered. Then the invaders flooded recklessly into the hushed town. Suddenly the Taipings who had concealed themselves behind the walls appeared and fought the enemy hand-to-hand with home-made guns and bamboo spears, killing a large number of them. Protet, the arrogant French admiral, was hit in the chest by a bullet and died immediately. The enemy troops pulled back, reorganized themselves and then finally captured the small market town. On May 20, they assailed the town of Chelin, meeting with the same resistance. Under heavy enemy fire, over 2,000 Taiping soldiers defended the town fiercely for a whole day, struggling for every inch of land until the last of them was dead. By then, the Anhwei Army had reached Shanghai under Li Hung-chang, an official who when he became prominent lined up with the invaders, taking foreign-made rifles and cannon from them to carry out massacres of the Chinese people.

Li Hung-chang, a native of Hofei in Anhwei, was a *chinshih*, i.e., a holder of the highest degree which could be gained through the imperial examination system. He venerated Tseng Kuo-fan as his teacher and served under him in the army. In the winter of 1861, the officials and merchants in Shanghai entreated Tseng Kuo-fan to send armed forces to protect them. Tseng Kuo-fan had just deployed his main force against the Heavenly Capital. Being anxious to win glory, he was most unwilling to break up this concentration, so he sent Li Hung-chang back to Anhwei to raise troops for what became known as the Anhwei Army. Formed in the spring of 1862, the Anhwei Army was modelled on the Hunan Army from which it also took some of its 7,000 officers and men. A number of its officers were from the landlords militia corps at Luan in Anhwei. Their hands had long been stained with the blood of revolution-aries. In April, the Sino-Foreign Defence Alliance in Shanghai hired seven British steamers which, under the convoy of British warships, transported this new counter-revolutionary army in batches down the Yangtze past the Heavenly Capital to Shanghai. Such was the origin of the Anhwei

Army which followed the Hunan Army in the development of the warlord forces in modern Chinese history. A month after his arrival in Shanghai, Li Hung-chang was appointed Governor of Kiangsu on Tseng Kuo-fan's recommendation.

In co-ordination with the newly-arrived Anhwei Army the invaders launched violent attacks on the Taiping Army capturing some of its strongholds outside Shanghai. But in the latter half of May, the Taipings began a large-scale counter-attack. They won a battle at Taitsang capturing more than 30 enemy strongholds, drove the British general Staveley out of Chiating and recaptured it. In his memorial to the Emperor, Li Hung-chang exposing the invaders' weakness, said that Chiating had fallen again, because the Western forces frightened by the rebels feared combat with them. In June, the Taiping Army under Tan Shao-kuang took Chingpu. Ward and a British army officer who rushed their troops from Sungkiang to give aid were beaten and fled to their camp with only a few men and horses and a little military equipment. The Taipings captured Forrester, the second-in-command of the "Ever-Victorious Army." Tso Tsung-tang said these two battles showed "the foreigners are as much scared of the long-haired rebels as we are." After taking Chingpu, 50,000-

60,000 Taipings laid siege to Shanghai once more, pushing forward to Fahuachen and Hsuchiahui. Their vanguard neared the "concessions" and the county town itself and fought bitter engagements in the areas around Hsuchiahui, Chiulichiao, Hsinchiao and Hungchiao with losses. Just at this moment, Hung Hsiu-chuan ordered the army back to support the capital which, hard-pressed by the Hunan Army, was in a critical situation. Leaving some troops in the vicinity of Shanghai, the main force of the Taiping Army marched away to the west and thus ended their advance on Shanghai.

The Taiping Army launched a furious attack against the invaders on the Chekiang front. Ningpo, one of the ports opened after the Treaty of Nanking, had been taken as a base on the Chekiang coast by the invaders. Four British vessels and two French ones moored in front of the "concessions" on the north side of the river with a large armed force on board. Following the pattern of Ward's "Ever-Victorious Army," the British consul recruited a mixed Sino-British force. Later, Prosper Giguel, a French customs commissioner at Ningpo, also set up a Sino-French force, the so-called "Ever-Triumphant Army."

Thus the invaders organized their forces here just as they had in Shanghai.

When Li Shih-hsien, the Prince Shih, attacked Ningpo in December 1861, the foreign invaders attempted to interfere. The subsequent occupation of Ningpo by the Taiping Army was a serious irritation to them, and in April-May of 1862, Roderick Dew, a British naval captain, acting on instructions from Admiral Hope, insolently issued an ultimatum to the Taipings to dismantle their gun positions on the city walls on the pretext that shells had fallen into the "concessions." The Taipings rejected these provocations in strong terms. The invaders, in concert with the Ching troops, began to shell the city with heavy cannon. The Taipings withstood this bravely, fighting fiercely for five hours. When the invading troops used ladders to scale the city walls, the Taipings met them head-on wounding two British officers and killing a French naval captain. The Taipings only withdrew from the city when all their principal generals had been seriously wounded. Of this occupation, even the *Hong-kong Daily Press* recorded: "There never was a falser, more unprovoked, or more unjustifiable act than the taking of Ningpo by the allies from the Taipings."*

* Quoted by Lin-le, p. 538.

In order to expand their intervention in Chekiang, the invaders transferred Ward's "Ever-Victorious Army" to the east Chekiang front. In the Tzehsi Battle of September 1862, Ward was hit when raising his head from behind a shelter, and within 24 hours this American aggressor was dead. The "Ever-Victorious Army" then retreated to Shanghai. Ward's death was a real blow to the invaders; the British consul in Shanghai wrote to his superior saying that they felt worried and hopeless about it because they did not know where to seek his successor. After Ward's death, the Taipings also killed A. E. Le Brethon and Tardif de Moidrey, the commanders of the Sino-French "Ever-Triumphant Army" at Shaohsing. Many other criminal aggressors also received their just deserts.

Ward was succeeded as commander of the "Ever-Victorious Army" by Henry Burgevine, Burgevine by Captain J. Y. Holland, and Holland by another British aggressor Charles George Gordon. Gordon had taken part in the joint Anglo-French invasion of Peking in 1860 and had led the criminal expedition which plundered and burned the Yuan Ming Yuan Summer Palace. Even he admitted that they had committed the most barbaric outrage in "destroying in a vandal-like manner most valuable property."* Gordon was a villainous capitalist felon.

Although foreign intervention caused the Taiping Army great difficulties, and finally had the gravest consequences, the unyielding heroes of the Heavenly Kingdom were not intimidated by the brutal invaders, but fought them to the bitter end.

* A. E. Hake: *Gordon in China and the Soudan*, London, 1896, p. 18.

By 1862 the military situation had turned against the Taipings, and their difficulties were increasing all the time.

Early that year, Tseng Kuo-fan, already an Imperial Commissioner and Viceroy of the Liangkiang Provinces, was appointed Assistant Grand Secretary and with these new powers he took charge of the military campaign against the Taipings in the whole of southeast China. He implemented his overall counter-revolutionary strategy step by step. The army on the central front led by Tseng Kuo-chuan began a siege of the Heavenly Capital in May that year. The Anhwei Army under Li Hung-chang which, after the withdrawal of the main Taiping force from Shanghai, had with aid from the foreign aggressors increased its numbers and improved its equipment was now the dominant force on the eastern front. The southern front under Tso Tsungtang in Chekiang was also steadily strengthened by foreign aid and had soon got the whole Chekiang front under control. This deployment of forces was designed to obliterate the Heavenly Capital and the power of the Taiping Army in Kiangsu and Chekiang.

Fighting on two fronts, struggling with both the Anhwei Army and the invaders in the east to try to defend their capital from that direction, while simultaneously fighting in the west to break through the encirclement of the capital and bring it succour, the Taipings could do little more than respond passively to the situation. They withdrew their forces from the Shanghai front and transferred them to the region around the capital in June and July 1862, gathering a large force of 200,000 men which made a frontal assault on Tseng Kuochuan's great camp at Yuhuatai. In the heavy fighting which lasted 46 days, although they hit the Hunan Army hard, Tseng Kuo-chuan was wounded, they failed to break through the enemy lines, so a stalemate resulted. In November, the Taipings were forced to retreat from this front around Yuhuatai because of heavy casualties and the onset of a bitter winter for which they lacked suitable clothing. Since the Taipings had mustered most of their fire-power for the attack at Yuhuatai and failed to break through, hope of smashing the encirclement of the Heavenly Capital became fainter and fainter.

The year in which the main forces of the Taiping Army were transferred west was one of great change on the Kiangsu and Chekiang battlefronts.

In Kiangsu, after the Taipings withdrew their main forces from the Shanghai area, the Chinese and foreign counter-revolutionary forces had made readjustments. Li Hung-chang had command not only of the Anhwei Army, but also of the local troops and the "Ever-Victorious Army," and was responsible for military affairs against the revolution along the line from Soochow and Changchow to Shanghai. This command arrangement shows the close co-operation and interdependence between the Chinese and foreign reactionaries. Nevertheless, the Taiping soldiers who had been left on the eastern front under Tan Shao-kuang advanced once more to Fahuaszu and Peihsinching on the edge of Shanghai at the end of August, 1862, and made attacks in Chiating in October. The odds were too great, and Tan Shao-kuang was finally forced to retreat. Still, in this last courageous struggle, his dauntless perseverance demonstrated his strong revolutionary spirit.

In January 1863, Lo Kuo-chung, the garrison commander at Changshu turned traitor and surrendered the city to Li Hung-chang, thus giving the enemy a foothold from which to attack southern Kiangsu. Subsequently, having taken Taitsang and Kunshan, they began to press on Soochow. Hung Hsiu-chuan was very worried by the deteriorating situation in southern Kiangsu. He issued a solemn proclamation to the whole army: "Every soldier should fight bravely with the enemy and the foreign troops allied with them." "Don't wait till a greater catastrophe befalls us."

In July, Li Hung-chang ordered all his troops and Gordon's "Ever-Victorious Army" to march on Soochow from Kunshan. They divided their forces and directed the northern group to take Kiangyin and Wusih while the southern group took Wukiang. Wukiang and Kiangyin fell one after the other, and by late August the enemy was hard by Soochow. In September, they laid siege to Wusih to cut the Taipings off from their rear and extend the encirclement of Soochow. Li Hung-chang hastened from Shanghai to direct the Soochow front. Under the command of Tan Shao-kuang, the Taipings at Soochow held out courageously, fighting furiously in its defence. They kept the Anhwei Army and the "Ever-Victorious Army" out of the solidly fortified city, leaving them to fight a wasting battle. On November 27, the "Ever-Victorious Army" under

Gordon made a night assault on the fort outside the Loumen Gate of the city and suffered 200 casualties for its pains. Seeing that a military victory was impossible, Li Hung-chang and Gordon tried to talk the Taipings into capitulation. On November 22, Gordon presumptuously wrote to the loyal Prince Mu, Tan Shao-kuang, trying to induce him to surrender. Tan Shao-kuang answered these underhand tactics with another ferocious onslaught. Tan Shao-kuang himself participated in this night battle in which Gordon's "Ever-Victorious Army" was utterly defeated. On 28, Li Hsiu-cheng, arriving from the Heavenly Capital, suggested that they abandon Soochow, but Tan Shao-kuang in firm opposition to such defeatism advocated keeping up the defensive battle to the end. In the meantime, some of the other generals at Soochow like Kao Yung-kuan and Wang An-chun were already preparing to defect. Although in command, Li Hsiu-cheng not only did nothing about this serious matter, when he learnt of it, he even said: "You must do as you please. We ought not to hurt each other. . . . At present, I can't hold you back. . . . I am a famous general in our country. Would anyone accept my surrender and protect me from danger?" Kao Yung-kuan and his group were very grateful and replied: "Prince Chung, please rest assured. We will never show ingratitude to you."* This meant that though they were going to surrender they would not do Li Hsiu-cheng any harm. This treasonous exchange revealed Li Hsiu-cheng's true nature. It showed what course he would take at this critical moment for the Taiping Heavenly Kingdom. On the evening of November 30, Li Hsiu-cheng, thinking that everything was over, abandoned tens of thousands of men and fled to the Heavenly Capital with a handful of his intimates.

Inside the city of Soochow, treachery was spreading fast. On December 4, Tan Shao-kuang called a meeting at his official residence hoping to save the situation. At the meeting, he spoke sincerely and with spirit, saying that they should fight to the last drop of blood. As he argued fiercely with the traitors, Wang An-chun suddenly unsheathed his sword and stabbed him. On December 5, Kao Yung-kuan, Wang An-chun and six other traitors welcomed the Ching troops into the city, offering them Tan Shao-kuang's head as they opened the city gate. They had hoped to save their own lives by thus presenting the enemy with the head of their comrade-in-arms, but in vain, for they were all executed by Li Hung-chang the next day. Thanks to

---

* See Li Hsiu-cheng's confession.

145

their treachery, over 20,000 Taiping soldiers were brutally murdered by Li Hung-chang at Soochow.

After the fall of Soochow, the decisive engagement of the south Kiangsu battlefield was fought in and around Changchow. In the defensive battle at Changchow and Chintan, the Taiping heroes struck hard at the troops of the Sino-foreign counter-revolutionary alliance. Gordon was seriously wounded and narrowly escaped death. These heroic struggles could not, however, save the whole war situation. In May 1864, Changchow, the Taipings' last stronghold in the south Kiangsu area fell.

Meanwhile, in Chekiang, after the Ching troops and the foreign invading forces had taken Ningpo in May 1862, Tso Tsung-tang led his Hunan troops down the Chientang River to its lower reaches, and the Taipings suffered one defeat after another. In the summer of 1863, Tso Tsung-tang besieged Fuyang, where the Taipings held out stubbornly for five months. It fell in September to a joint attack by Tso Tsung-tang's troops and the "Ever-Triumphant Army" under P. A. Neveue d'Aiguebelle. Fuyang was the most important fortified point south of Hangchow, and after its fall, Tso Tsung-tang joined forces with the "Ever-Triumphant Army" to invade Hangchow.

Between October and November, the Taipings fought bitterly with Tso's troops and the "Ever-

Triumphant Army" in the area between Hangchow and Yuhang and on the outskirts of Hangchow. On November 28, they took advantage of a dense fog to storm Tso's camp from Wansungling. Unfortunately, Soochow fell early in December with adverse repercussions for the defence of Hangchow, which was finally captured by Tso Tsung-tang late in March 1864. By then, except for Huchow and a few other strongholds all Chekiang was under Ching control.

The loss of all the cities and towns of Kiangsu and Chekiang left no room for manoeuvre around the perimeter of the Heavenly Capital, and no possible base from which aid might be given. The Taiping Heavenly Kingdom was in the greatest danger. Meanwhile, Li Hung-chang, Tso Tsung-tang and their like were being rewarded with high government positions for killing thousands of revolutionary people. Li Hung-chang was granted the title of Junior Guardian to the Heir Apparent when he captured Soochow. Before leading his troops to Hangchow, Tso Tsung-tang was appointed Viceroy of Fukien and Chekiang. Their underlings were all awarded with posts as provincial military commanders or divisional commanders. In order to show his gratitude to his foreign masters, after the capture of Changchow, Li Hung-chang memorialized the Emperor asking him to reward Gordon, the villainous foreign butcher of the Chinese people, not only by giving him the rank of *titu,* or general, but also granting him the right to wear the Yellow Riding Jacket and the double-eyed peacock feather, symbols of rank within the imperial bureaucracy. Nothing could more clearly demonstrate the ugly collaboration of the domestic reactionaries with the foreign aggressors to suppress the Chinese revolution.

On December 4, 1863, after the fall of Soochow, Li Hsiu-cheng returned to the Heavenly Capital to supervise its defence, but he felt gloomy and hopeless about the future of the revolution. The capital was surrounded and the tension increased day by day. Hung Hsiu-chuan called on all the troops and civilians within the walls to stand together bravely in united resistance.

Meanwhile, in order to gain the initiative, the Taiping Army in the Kiangsu-Chekiang battlefield kept trying to break out of their encirclement. At the beginning of February 1864, the first group of around 80,000 marched from Liyang in Kiangsu and Kuangteh and Ningkuo in Anhwei through the Tienmu Mountains and on to the Fukien-Kiangsi border areas. The second group of about 200,000 under the command of Li Shih-hsien, the Prince

Shih, left Teching in Chekiang for Kiangsi. This had quite an effect. The enemy, really upset by the movements of the Taiping Army, complained fearfully that every time they took one place they lost another, and that they were tired of rushing about. Unfortunately the Taipings did not take the chance to attack the enemy troops, so they gained a breathing space in which reinforcements were brought in, and the Kiangsi defences were strengthened. When the third group of around 30,000 broke through the encirclement at Tanyang and marched through southern Anhwei to Kiangsi, it met serious opposition. The group's losses were heavy, and only a part of it continued south to join forces with Li Shih-hsien. The Taiping armies which broke through the encirclement in Kiangsu and Chekiang drew off part of the main force of the Hunan troops, somewhat reducing the pressure on the Heavenly Capital but, as the Taipings did not follow this up with any positive military measures, the general situation remained disadvantageous.

Tseng Kuo-chuan, planning to intensify the attack, enlisted new recruits bringing the number of Hunan troops encircling the capital to 50,000 men.

On February 28, 1864, Tienpaocheng, a stronghold in the Chungshan Mountains outside the capital, fell. On March 2, the enemy assailed the Taiping and Shentse gates in the northeastern part of the city wall. The encirclement drew ever tighter. The capital was running short of food, and conditions there were very difficult. Li Hsiu-cheng reported to Hung Hsiu-chuan: "There is no food in the whole city, a great number of men and women have died." He asked Hung Hsiu-chuan to issue a decree on arrangements "so that the people might be reassured." Showing his absolute determination that they should fight to the last, Hung Hsiu-chuan said that the whole city should live on grass.

As there was no more grain in the city, Li Hsiu-cheng suggested allowing the townspeople to leave. Hung Hsiu-chuan opposed this demoralizing measure and he castigated Li Hsiu-cheng for "daring to ignore the dignity of a nation by letting our brothers and sisters out to wander around." Recalcitrant, though outwardly compliant, Li Hsiu-cheng forced through a secret order to permit the townspeople to flee. Later, in his confession, Li Hsiu-cheng even boasted of this and lavished praises on the enemy. He said: "In the city I learned that the Marshal [Tseng Kuo-chuan] had established a bureau to aid refugees. . . . This accorded with my idea . . . and I . . . ordered they be allowed to go. Since last year, not less than 130,000 or 140,000 people have left by the various gates."* (This number is inaccurate, and probably very exaggerated.)

---

* See Li Hsiu-cheng's confession.

Inside the capital, the Taiping soldiers were united in their resolution to live or die with the Heavenly Capital. In this dauntless spirit, they put up a determined defence. In spite of the long siege, the enemy could not overcome this revolutionary bulwark. In April, Tseng Kuo-chuan twice ordered the whole army to dig tunnels and make scaling ladders to assail the city but they were met head-on and thrown back.

Long tension and exertion had led to a steady decline in Hung Hsiu-chuan's health and he finally succumbed to illness and died on June 1, 1864. His death was a terrible loss for the Taiping Heavenly Kingdom in the last stage of its struggles.

Hung Hsiu-chuan was a revolutionary leader of the peasantry in semi-colonial and semi-feudal China, and also a prominent revolutionary forerunner in the early period of the old democratic revolution. The Taiping Revolution which he led was of great significance in the history of modern China. He struggled unremittingly against enemies from inside and outside the country, devoted himself to the service of the people to the last, contributing his life to their revolutionary cause. Chairman Mao has said: **"For a hundred years, the finest sons and daughters of the disaster-ridden Chinese nation fought and sacrificed their lives, one stepping into** the breach as another fell, in quest of the truth that would save the country and the people. This moves us to song and tears."* Hung Hsiu-chuan is just such an outstanding character worthy of our remembrance. He represented the demands and aspirations of the people of his time and reflected the progressive trend of history.

After the death of Hung Hsiu-chuan, the Taiping Heavenly Kingdom was in mortal danger. Hung Hsiu-chuan's elder son, the 16-year-old Hung Tien-kuei-fu, succeeded his father as Heavenly King. At this time, Hung Jen-kan had left the city to seek grain and reinforcements. As the whole area was short of food, he found nothing and did not return. Even in this crisis, the soldiers defending the capital fought bravely on and kept the enemy out of the city.

During the long defence of the capital, after the death of Chen Yu-cheng, Chen Teh-tsai, the Prince Foo, and Lai Wen-kuang, the Prince Tsun, had led their troops to the northwest, and they were active around Hanchung in Shensi. In the spring of 1864, hearing of the dangerous situation which had arisen, Chen Teh-tsai and Lai Wen-kuang led their men back from Shensi to save the Heavenly Capital. In April this army entered Hupeh from Honan. The

---

* Mao Tsetung: Vol. III, p. 17.

Nien troops in Honan under Chen Ta-hsi and those in Anhwei under Chang Tsung-yu joined forces with the Taiping Army. The rapidly-expanding force became a threat to the Ching troops besieging the capital. To prevent the Taipings moving eastwards, the Ching government hurriedly built up defensive lines in Hupeh, mainly relying on Sengalintsin's cavalry, but also transferring troops from Honan, Hupeh, Anhwei and other provinces and positioning them prepared for battle along the foot of the Tapieh Mountains. At the same time, the Ching government seriously reprimanded Tseng Kuo-chuan for his failure to capture the Heavenly Capital. In June and July it sent Li Hung-chang six orders in succession commanding him to hasten to assist Tseng Kuo-chuan with the attack on the Heavenly Capital. Li Hung-chang, however, held back knowing that the two brothers Tseng Kuo-fan and Tseng Kuo-chuan would be jealous if someone else snatched away their glory. Tseng Kuo-chuan then made great efforts to take the capital as quickly as possible, and the fighting there consequently intensified. It was a bitter struggle in which the enemy paid dearly for each step forward.

On July 3, Tipaocheng, another stronghold on the capital's defence perimeter on the third peak of the Chungshan Mountains fell. This gave the enemy control of the high land overlooking the whole city, a deterioration in the situation which inaugurated the last stage of the battle. On July 4, Tseng Kuo-chuan savagely ordered his various battalions to attack the city in rotation day and night.

The Taipings continued to hold out in the isolated city with utmost bravery. Their determination to win, and their refusal to yield to anyone still frightened the enemy. In a memorial to the Emperor, Tseng Kuo-fan said that the difficulty of attacking the city and the bitter fighting were "such as had never been experienced even by the veteran fighters." "We try hundreds of ways to attack and still find no weakness of which we can take advantage." "Each battalion attacks in turn, leaving many dead and wounded." "Over 50,000 officers and men all worn out and exhausted." "Something else may happen if the fight goes on, and if so, how dreadful it would be."

The heroic Taiping soldiers, cut off from all help and struggling against great odds, held out for a fortnight until only 3,000 to 4,000 defenders survived. On July 18, Tseng Kuo-chuan put on his armour, went to the mouth of a tunnel and directed his men to lay 15,000 kilogrammes of dynamite. Two columns of Taiping Army, each of several hundred men, sallied out from the Taiping and Chaoyang gates armed with fire-balls and set fire to the artillery posts and their stores of hay.

Taken by surprise the Ching troops fought back, and only saved the mouth of their tunnel by a desperate fight. At noon on July 19, the enemy blew a breach in the city wall over 60 metres wide, and began to swarm through it. Taiping soldiers on the city wall fought bravely, throwing down gunpowder which drove the Ching troops back until their officers forced them on again by drawing their swords and slaying those who dared to retreat. By dusk after hours of fierce combat, the Ching troops had broken through at every gate.

The heroic defenders of the Heavenly Capital struggled over every inch of land in the city, fighting for the revolution in hand-to-hand combat with the enemy until they all fell. Even the enemy had to admit that not one of the Taiping soldiers in the city had surrendered. In sacrificing their lives these heroes created the most tragic and moving passage in the history of the Taiping Heavenly Kingdom.

After the reactionary troops had captured the Heavenly Capital they really revealed their brutal nature. An eye-witness said: "When the Hunan troops got into the city, they killed everyone they met, burned every house they saw, seized young women and looted valuables." This is an accurate summary of their savage behaviour. Tseng Kuochuan led the pillage of the Palace of the Heavenly

King while other commanders rushed to ransack the rest of the city. After carrying off their plunder, they put everything to the flame. Soon the blaze lit up the sky and the air was heavy with smoke which did not disperse as the fire burned for seven days. The prosperous city was thus all at once reduced to ashes.

Li Hsiu-cheng and the young Heavenly King rushed out of the city as it fell, but were soon separated by the enemy troops. Li Hsiu-cheng fled eastwards to Fangshan, carrying with him gold, silver, pearls and precious stones. Then he was found by traitors and sent under guard to Tseng Kuo-chuan's camp. In the presence of the enemy, he meekly expressed repentance and beseeched that his life might be spared. On July 28, Tseng Kuo-fan hurried to Nanking from Anking and interrogated Li Hsiu-cheng. Li having abased himself completely before him, wrote a confession running into tens of thousands of words.

In his confession, the traitor Li Hsiu-cheng shamelessly praised Tseng Kuo-fan, the sworn enemy of the Taiping Heavenly Kingdom, viciously abused the Taiping Revolution and railed against himself for having been so stupid as to join it. Willing to sell out the revolution to save his own skin, he offered to persuade the Taiping troops to capitulate to the Ching dynasty. But Tseng Kuo-fan executed him on the very day he finished his confession. Thus perished an infamous traitor.

The fall of the Heavenly Capital marked the failure of the Taiping Revolution. Reactionaries were jubilant over the new appointments and honours with which they were rewarded. Tseng Kuo-fan was given the title of Grand Guardian to the Heir Apparent and made a Marquis of the First Class while Tseng Kuo-chuan became Junior Guardian to the Heir Apparent and Earl of the First Class decorated with the double-eyed peacock feather. All the leaders of the forces in the southeast were rewarded by the Ching government.

After the defeat of the revolution, the landlord class returned to take revenge. The feudal officials proposed various measures to the Ching government to protect the ownership of the landlords who had fled and to ensure the rapid restoration of the feudal land system which had been so damaged by the revolution. The Ching government ordered each province to restore the feudal order as soon as possible. The officials in various provinces in the lower Yangtze collaborated with the landlords to snatch land from the peasants. They worked out the so-called "identify and claim system for wasteland," which was in the charge of landlords and despotic gentry. Under the guise of "identification of wasteland," they snatched lands away from the peasants.

The procedure for identifying land was very simple: those who could show land deeds could occupy land, in other words, it was taken from the peasants and returned to its "original owners"; those without deeds to show could get the local official to issue a kind of certificate and then they could also occupy the peasants' land. The landlords or the so-called "original owners" seized land everywhere. Sometimes they collaborated with the officials to stir up trouble to serve as a pretext for taking people's land.

The fugitive landlords, especially those from southern Kiangsu, returned in a cruel mood. During the revolution they had fled with their riches to Shanghai or had hidden themselves in Nantung, Haimen, Chungming and other places at the mouth of the Yangtze, seeking the protection of the foreign aggressors. Now, they swarmed back to their old homes trying to obliterate every right gained by the peasants during the revolution.

The Struggle Goes On   14

After the fall of the Heavenly Capital, the young Heavenly King escaped to join Hung Jen-kan in Kuangteh, Anhwei. They arrived at Huchow in Chekiang in August 1864 and decided to go to Kiangsi to link up with Li Shih-hsien and Wang Hai-yang who had gone there with the remnants of their forces from the Kiangsu-Chekiang battlefield. Afterwards they planned to join Lai Wen-kuang in Hupeh whose army had left Shensi in the northwest to go to the aid of the capital, but had got no further than Hupeh when they were blockaded by Ching troops in April 1864. Together they thought their forces could then go to Shensi to reorganize and await further developments. Arriving in Kiangsi, however, they found that they had missed the Taiping Army under Li Shih-hsien and Wang Hai-yang, which had already gone to Fukien.

Hung Jen-kan and the young Heavenly King were captured soon afterwards, and sent to the provincial capital Nanchang to be executed. Hung Jen-kan fulfilled his oath: "I would rather sacrifice my life for the nation than live ignobly in oblivion." He met his death calmly and in his last poem he wrote that although the destiny of the Taiping Heavenly Kingdom had thus been cut short, it would one day be revived. This shows he still hoped that a new nation would be built.

After Li Shih-hsien led his forces to Fukien, they captured Changchow and some other places. He proclaimed a series of new policies and began to establish a base area. The Ching government, fearing that the Taipings would take a firm hold on Fukien, immediately sent Tso Tsung-tang there as an Imperial Commissioner to surround Changchow from three directions. Li Shih-hsien held out in an extremely difficult situation for six months, before he was defeated in May 1865. After three months of marching, he finally arrived at Wang Hai-yang's camp. Wang Hai-yang, suspecting Li Shih-hsien might reproach him for having failed to go to his aid when he was in danger, had Li Shih-hsien slain. Later, Wang Hai-yang's troops fought on the Kiangsi-Kwangtung border, capturing Chiaying (present-day Meihsien) in Kwangtung. In February

1866, Wang Hai-yang was killed in battle, and one of his generals, Tan Ti-yuan, captured when leading a charge through the encirclement, was executed.

Although the heroic struggles of the Taiping Army south of the Yangtze had come to an end, the Taiping Army and the Nien forces kept on fighting stubbornly north of the Yangtze.

At the end of 1864, the Nien fighters and the northwestern Taiping Army chose Lai Wen-kuang, the Taiping Prince Tsun, as their leader. Lai Wen-kuang reorganized the Nien forces in line with the Taiping system and proclaimed that they should carry on the revolutionary cause of the Taiping Heavenly Kingdom. They developed a vigorous armed struggle in the Yellow River valley.

At the beginning of 1865, Lai Wen-kuang, Chang Tsung-yu and others won a great victory over Sengalintsin at Lushan in Honan. Sengalintsin, a Mongol noble, was a favourite of the Ching court, and his Manchu-Mongol cavalry was exceedingly cruel. To annihilate this stubborn enemy, Lai Wen-kuang practised mobile warfare, "keeping the enemy on the move," first exhausting him and then taking the chance to wipe him out. This arrogant butcher Sengalintsin misinterpreting the Nien troops' mobile tactics, believed they were trying to escape and followed close at their heels for almost two months. Sometimes the Niens marched day and night covering 500 kilometres in a few days; sometimes they circled around within a 50-kilometre radius. Because of their flexible tactics, the Nien fighters would reach a place several days earlier than the weary Ching troops. The Nien fighters would zigzag east and west, north and south, exhausting the Ching troops. Every place which Sengalintsin reached, he found deserted. He was so tired that he could no longer hold the reins. On May 18, when the Ching army was pursuing the Nien fighters to Kaochuang in Tsaohsien County, Shantung Province, Lai Wen-kuang saw the time had come to act. He first stationed three columns before Kaochuang as a decoy, while hiding his main force in the willow grove outside the little town. Like a gambler who has lost his judgement, Sengalintsin charged wildly forward to slay his foes. Promptly the concealed Nien troops closed in around the enemy, meting out heavy punishment. In a state of great confusion, Sengalintsin attempted to flee. But there was no way out of that strong encirclement. The Nien fighters, whose hatred for this perpetrator of numerous atrocities was intense, gladly slew him.

Sengalintsin's whole army was annihilated to the great alarm of the Ching government, which feared that the Nien troops would cross to the north side of the Yellow River and press straight on to Peking. Tseng Kuo-fan was sent to deal with the situation. In order to avoid the exhaustion of pursuing the Nien troops, he adopted a strategy of gradual advance with the intention of blockading the highly mobile Nien fighters between the Grand Canal, the Shaho River, the Huai River and the Yellow River. This cunning plot was, however, never realized for, by the time Tseng Kuo-fan had reached Linhuai in Anhwei, the Nien fighters had already left Shantung and had entered Honan in two groups. Tseng Kuo-fan was repeatedly defeated and his encirclement strategy met with complete failure. The Ching government, seeing Tseng Kuo-fan's incompetence, replaced him with Li Hung-chang, the commander of the Anhwei Army.

Wishing to fight a protracted struggle and to develop the revolutionary forces, Lai Wen-kuang divided the Nien troops into an east column and a west column. At the end of 1866, Lai Wen-kuang led the east column to Hupeh, taking Huangpi, Hsiaokan, Yunmeng, Teh-an and other places. At the beginning of 1867 they lured a section of the Hunan Army under Kuo Sung-lin to Chiukouchen in Anlu (present-day Chunghsiang) and annihilated more than half of them in a quick decisive offensive at Lochiachi. Then in a surprise raid at Yinlungho (present-day Yunglungho), they caught and destroyed another column of Anhwei troops under Liu Ming-chuan just as it was crossing a river. Liu Ming-chuan and the other Ching commanders took off their armour and their helmets and sat on the ground waiting for death. Suddenly another column of Hunan troops arrived, shooting at the Nien fighters from the rear, and the Niens caught unprepared, retreated to Honan with heavy losses.

In June 1867, the east column of the Nien troops marched into Shantung but failed to break through the canal defence line built up by Li Hung-chang. Their range of activity began to diminish and they gradually forfeited the initiative. They lost their main force trying to force their way across the Liutang River and only over 2,000 men won through. After the breakthrough, Lai Wen-kuang was taken prisoner and was killed at Yangchow on January 10, 1868.

The west column of the Nien troops under Chang Tsung-yu prospered as it went from Honan to Shensi. Towards the end of 1866, when they were closing in on Sian, Liu Jung, a Ching official who had just been dismissed from the post of Governor of Shensi, led some Hunan troops against them from Huayin. The Nien troops, circling around Sian, Lantien and Lintung swooped down on them first from one direction, and then from another. At the beginning of 1867, the Nien fighters numbering 50,000 horsemen and infantry set an ambush at Shihlipo in Pachiao near Sian. When the Hunan troops went into the trap, they charged down on them from left and right. In only half a day they thus annihilated more than 30 enemy battalions.

The Shihlipo Battle weakened the Ching forces in Shensi. Tso Tsung-tang was immediately transferred there to bring the situation under control. The Nien fighters broke through the encirclement he set up, and pushed on to north Shensi where they took Ansai, Yenchuan, Suiteh and other cities, building up considerable power. In the meantime, news arrived of the east column's danger. In December 1867, the west column crossed the frozen Yellow River and pushed through Shansi to Yichow in Chihli with extraordinary speed, passing through three provinces in less than two months. Chang Tsung-yu had originally planned to take the pressure off the east column of the Nien troops by mounting a threat on Peking, but unfortunately the east column had been defeated a month before, so his troops were isolated in the enemy's midst.

In August 1868, the Nien fighters broke through to Chihping in Shantung where they were defeated in their final battle.

The Taiping heroes, together with the Nien fighters, had continued their steadfast struggle for nearly four years after the fall of the Heavenly Capital. They won many victories against great odds. Holding high the great banner of the Taiping Heavenly Kingdom, they struggled on for the revolutionary cause in its best traditions. They are worthy to be called the finest sons and daughters of the Chinese nation.

The Heroes of the Taiping Heavenly Kingdom Will Never Be Forgotten

The Taiping Revolution was the first great high tide of the revolution in the history of modern China. It lasted over 10 years and revolutionary power affected almost the whole country. None of the peasant wars of the past can compare with the Taiping Revolution in scope or influence. It set up the Pai Shang Ti Hui, a popular organization to lead the people in their revolutionary struggles. It formed, in the course of struggle, a whole set of political, economic, military, educational and cultural institutions. It founded its own state power, which stood and struggled for a considerable period against that of the Ching government. From the Pearl River to the Yangtze and the Yellow River, hundreds of millions of people were involved in this wave of revolution, one of the grandest and most remarkable events in Chinese history.

The behaviour of the Taiping revolutionaries when they mounted the stage of modern Chinese history was quite different from that of participants in earlier peasant revolutions. Not only did they struggle against feudalism, they also shouldered the task of opposing the aggressive forces of foreign capitalism. It was a revolution against imperialism and its lackeys, the Ching dynasty.

As everybody knows, the first eight decades of the 110 years of anti-imperialist, anti-feudal bourgeois-democratic revolution in China, made up the old democratic revolution and the last three, the new democratic revolution. The preparatory period for the old democratic revolution "**began with the Opium War in 1840, *i.e.*, when China's feudal society started changing into a semi-colonial and semi-feudal one.**"* The storm of the Taiping Revolution, already brewing around the time of the Opium War, broke out nine years afterwards. At that time national and class contradictions were the basic contradictions in China's society, and history had already given the Chinese people the twofold task of opposing imperialism and opposing feudalism. Obviously, the background against which the Taiping Revolution was played out, differed from the background of the pure peasant

---

* Mao Tsetung: Vol. II, p. 342.

wars of the past. In the preparatory period of the bourgeois-democratic revolution, the tasks of the revolutionary peasant war were heavier and it also had new prospects. Between the 1840s and the 1860s, the invasion of foreign capitalist economy and the development of the domestic commodity economy brought certain splits within the landlord and peasant classes — originally the opposed classes in Chinese society. A new class force was about to emerge. Obvious signs of this can be found throughout the history of the Taiping Revolution.

Before the Chintien Uprising, Hung Hsiu-chuan had expressed his political and historical point of view. He said: "Though I haven't joined the San Ho Hui, I am told that it aims at opposing the Ching dynasty and restoring the Ming dynasty. This was quite all right at the time of the Kang Hsi Emperor* when this Society was founded. Now, 200 years have elapsed, to talk of opposing the Ching is still correct, but to talk of restoring the Ming is no longer correct. Anyhow . . . a new dynasty should be created. How can we have any appeal for the people if we keep the slogan of restoring the Ming?" Hung Hsiu-chuan was the earliest of the progressive Chinese who looked to

---

* The second emperor of the Ching dynasty, who reigned from 1662 to 1722.

the West for truth. This is clearer still if we see these words of his together with the many documents of the Taiping Heavenly Kingdom. These, for example, frequently raise such ideas as the equality of man and equality between the sexes. The *Heavenly Land System* was actually a plan to give "land to the tillers." The *New Guide to Government* was a blueprint for building a capitalist society. All these prove that the "new dynasty" Hung Hsiu-chuan planned to set up was no mere repetition of the old change of dynasties but would have transformed the feudal system and opened up a new road.

The Ching government, however, was already a tool for aggression in the hands of Britain, France, Russia, America and other Western capitalist countries. The foreign invaders feared that should the Chinese people overthrow the Ching government, the interests they had gained through aggression would be forfeited, so no sooner had the Taipings established their political power, before they had had the chance to carry out their great ideal, the invaders conspired with the Ching ruling class to strangle the Taiping Revolution. Chairman Mao, in summing up the historical lessons of China's democratic revolution, has pointed out: **"Earlier revolutions failed in China because**

imperialism strangled them, and innumerable revolutionary martyrs died, bitterly lamenting the non-fulfilment of their mission."* The heroes of the Taiping Heavenly Kingdom from Hung Hsiu-chuan to Chen Yu-cheng, Hung Jen-kan, Tan Shao-kuang and Lai Wen-kuang all died with this bitterness in their hearts.

Feudal power combined with the aggressive strength of the foreign capitalists to make a strong reactionary force. The magnificent Taiping movement was after all a peasant revolutionary movement. As the peasants were small producers, they could not by themselves repel the combined onslaughts of foreign capitalist aggression and domestic feudal power. The peasant masses want liberation and dare to engage in armed struggle to gain it, but in the midst of success, they are easily carried away and do not see the revolution through to the end. During the triumphant days when the capital was established at Nanking, bad old habits like conservatism, pleasure-seeking and factionalism besieged the revolutionary ranks. The Taiping heroes, who never flinched before the terrors of war, lost the strength to hit back under the onslaught of decadent feudal habits, which

---

* Mao Tsetung: Vol. II, p. 354.

brought disaster to the revolutionary cause of the Taiping Heavenly Kingdom.

Because of the historical conditions prevailing in China at that time, with the new class force still waiting to be born, the Taiping Revolution could not benefit from the leadership of the Chinese working class and its Party, so it could neither overcome its own weaknesses, nor completely formulate the strategy and tactics with which to vanquish the enemy. In spite of its great revolutionary influence and many victories, it was inevitably defeated in the end. The failure of the Taiping Revolution illustrates the dictum that **"without the leadership of the working class revolution fails."***

Although the Taiping Revolution failed, its marvellous contribution to the forward march of history will last forever.

From the first moment of its existence, the Taiping Heavenly Kingdom directed its attack against the feudal ruling class represented by the Ching dynasty and against the foreign capitalist aggressors. In taking on this anti-imperialist, anti-feudal role it prepared the way for the democratic revolution. Its militant history has been a constant source of inspiration to the Chinese people in their revolutionary struggles.

---

* Mao Tsetung: Vol. IV, p. 421.

The Taiping Revolution battered the superstructure of the feudal society. The supreme ruler of the feudal nation was the emperor, "a born sage" whom nobody could oppose. Hung Hsiu-chuan regarded all the sinister forces as "monsters and devils" and the emperor, as "Monster King of Hell." Not only their enemy, the Ching emperor, but all emperors in history were "Monster Kings of Hell." He said in his *Doctrines on Arousing the World*: "In the 1,000-2,000 years [sic] since the Chin and Han dynasties, the spirits of ordinary people have been tortured and persecuted by the Monster Kings of Hell." This was an indirect negation of monarchical dictatorship, opposition to which became a key point in the bourgeois democratic revolution in 1911. The Taipings had the courage to depose Confucius, the spiritual idol eulogized as the "Ultimate Sage and Foremost Teacher" by the feudal ruling class in the past dynasties. They said that the Confucian code was worth nothing, and condemned the "Four Books" and the "Five Classics"* of the Confucian school as "books of sorcery." They condemned feudal

---

* The "Four Books" are *The Great Learning, Doctrine of the Mean, Analects* and *The Works of Mencius.* The "Five Classics" are *The Book of Odes, The Book of Documents, The Book of Change, The Book of Rites* and *The Spring and Autumn Annals.*

174

literature on the teachings of the "sages," and so in a sense heralded the new culture movement in the May 4th period (1919) with its slogan of "Down with the Confucian Shop." It is true that the Taiping Revolution made use of the religious doctrines of the Pai Shang Ti Hui to hammer at the chains of feudalism, but they did so because no adequate critical weapon was as yet available to them. In doing so, however, they changed the enslaving Christian doctrines into a philosophy of rebellion with which they struck hard at the stubbornly fortified reactionary feudal superstructure. And the blow went home. Did not Tseng Kuo-fan bewail that "Confucius and Mencius are weeping in the underworld?"

The Taipings sought to transform the feudal system of landownership and the face of feudal society by building an ideal society where people were equal. Though only a beautiful design, this was a serious challenge to the whole of feudal society. In actual struggle when the Taipings occupied a place, they overthrew the local political power of the Ching dynasty. They burned land contracts and title deeds and killed or drove away the bureaucrats and landlords. The peasants seized back large areas of land, dealing a heavy blow to the feudal economic base. The result of this blow could be seen in the increased numbers of peasants who owned their own land in the lower Yangtze regions, in spite of the vengeful counter-attacks which the landlord class did later launch. For instance, in 1869, it was proclaimed in Kiangsu that henceforth the cultivator might claim owner-less land and would possess it in perpetuity as soon as an official certificate was granted. As the pre-fectural cities of Kiangning and Chenkiang were comparatively severely hit by the revolution, quite a lot of small holders obtained their land rights by tilling ownerless land. Other peasants who bought small pieces of land became small holders. In 1869, Ma Hsin-yi, Viceroy of the Liangkiang Provinces, said in a memorial to the throne that there had recently been a shortage of people to work the land in the lower Yangtze, and wasteland was usually sold at a low price. He said people bought waste-land as their own property to till themselves or to hire out to tenants to cultivate. Conditions in Anhwei and Chekiang were about the same. In some places in Chekiang, most of the land became the property of the small holders. In Tunghsiang County, for example, there were about 10,000 small holders who owned less than 10 *mu* each. In Lungyu County, after the changes wrought by the revolution, the majority of those engaged in farming were settlers and most of their land was former wasteland transferred to them as the cultivators. In Tanghsi County, the rich became bankrupt, and the land fell into the hands of former tenant farmers, of whom about seven or eight out of 10 owned and cultivated their land themselves. All this proves that the anti-feudal struggles of the Taipings produced certain changes in the relations of production in the rural areas. This change, the increase of the owner-cultivators, was beneficial to the promotion of a commodity economy. Much of the landlord class after the experience of the revolution regarded landownership as holding little promise, so they invested part of their capital in industry and commerce, where it became a source of national capital. The comparatively rapid development of capitalist economy in the middle and lower Yangtze later on was partly due to the fact that the Taiping Heavenly Kingdom had broken the rigid barriers of feudalism.

The Taiping Heavenly Kingdom fought persistently against the barbaric invasion of the foreign capitalists, firmly refused all their unreasonable demands and resisted their armed intervention with determination. These facts **"all testify to the Chinese people's indomitable spirit in fighting imperialism and its lackeys."***

---

* Mao Tsetung: Vol. II, p. 314.

The Taiping Revolution failed. But its brilliant deeds and its marvellous contribution to history will live forever in people's memories. Lenin said: **"Marx was also able to appreciate that there are moments in history when a desperate struggle of the *masses*, even for a hopeless cause, is *essential* for the further schooling of these masses and their training for the *next* struggle."*** The great struggles of the Taiping Revolution propelled history forward and inspired those who came later to take the revolutionary course of overthrowing those lackeys of imperialism — the Ching rulers.

The martyrs of the Taiping Heavenly Kingdom will never be forgotten.

---

* Lenin: "Preface to the Russian Translation of Karl Marx's Letters to Dr. Kugelmann."

Index

Alcock, John Rutherford, 100
America, *see* United States
American Baptist Church, 87
Anhwei Army (淮军), 133-135, 140-141, 142, 143, 164, 165
Aplin, 129

Bible, 15, 22
Bonham, George, 100, 101, 102
Bourboulon, Alphonse de, 101, 102, 105, 127
Britain (British), 1, 2, 3, 4, 14, 52, 91, 99, 100, 101, 102, 103,
   104, 105, 108, 113, 115, 126-127, 129, 130, 131, 132, 134, 135,
   136, 137, 138, 171
British Museum, 116
Bruce, Frederick, 105
Burgevine, Henry, 106, 131, 138

Catholics, 15, 102
Chai Chiao (斋教), 9
Chang Chao (张钊), 11
Chang Chia-hsiang (张嘉祥), 10
Chang Kuo-liang (张国梁), 67, 71, 95, 97, 98

Northern Prince (北王), *see* Wei Chang-hui

official examinations, 13, 14, 15, 16, 134
opium, 1-2, 4, 8
Opium War, 1, 4, 5, 6, 9, 13, 14, 16, 169

Pai Lien Chiao (白莲教), 9
Pai Shang Ti Hui (拜上帝会), 12, 17, 22-26, 28, 29, 87, 168, 175
Palmerston, 126
Pao Chao (鲍超), 117
Parkes, Harry, 113, 114
Peng Ta-shun (彭大顺), 79
political administration, 50-52
prefecture (*fu*) (府), 64
Prince An (安王), *see* Hung Jen-fa
Prince Chung (忠王), *see* Li Hsiu-cheng
Prince Foo (扶王), *see* Chen Teh-tsai
Prince Fu (福王), *see* Hung Jen-ta
Prince Kan (干王), *see* Hung Jen-kan
Prince Kung (恭亲王), 127-128
Prince Mu (慕王), *see* Tan Shao-kuang
Prince Shih (侍王), *see* Li Shih-hsien
Prince Tsun (遵王), *see* Lai Wen-kuang
Prince Yen (燕王), *see* Chin Jih-kang
Prince Yi (翼王), *see* Shih Ta-kai
Prince Ying (英王), *see* Chen Yu-cheng
Protestant, 14
Protet, A. L., 132, 133

Roberts, Issachar J., 21, 22
Russell, John, 105
Russia, 104, 171